The Italian Renaissance

by
Karen Osman

Lucent Books, P.O. Box 289011, San Diego, CA 92198-9011

Library of Congress Cataloging-in-Publication Data

Osman, Karen, 1955–
    The Italian Renaissance / by Karen Osman.
        p. cm.—(World history series)
    Includes bibliographical references and index.
    Summary: Examines the history, achievements, and legacy
of the Renaissance in Italy, with an emphasis on Florence
and Rome.
    ISBN 1-56006-237-1   (alk. paper)
    1. Renaissance—Italy—Juvenile literature.   2. Italy—
Civilization—1268-1559—Juvenile literature. [1. Renaissance
—Italy.   2. Italy—Civilization—1268-1559.]   I.Title.
II. Series.
DG445.075   1996
945'.05—dc20   95-31679
                                                        CIP
                                                        AC

This book is lovingly dedicated to the memory of my dear and
trusted friend
Ken Terrill
(February 23, 1955–March 24, 1994)
and to
Doug Wilkie
whose love, strength, and devotion will always serve as my
model for what is right and good in the world.

Acknowledgments

The author would like to gratefully acknowledge the help of
Jacqueline A. Bober, Catherine M. Jennings, and Jeff Parsons.
Without their expertise in the areas of history and art history
this book could not have been written. Special thanks are also
due to Gene Mittler, Ph.D., for his interpretation of
Parmigianino's *Madonna with the Long Neck.*

Contents

Foreword   6

Important Dates in the History of the
Italian Renaissance   8

INTRODUCTION
A Bridge in Time   10

CHAPTER 1
The Seeds of the Italian Renaissance   13

CHAPTER 2
The Early Renaissance in Florence   25

CHAPTER 3
Humanism in the Early Renaissance   34

CHAPTER 4
Art and Architecture of the Early Renaissance   44

CHAPTER 5
Rome and French Invasions of Italy   56

CHAPTER 6
Three Great Artists of the High Renaissance   69

CHAPTER 7
The Late Renaissance   81

CONCLUSION
Afterimage   92

Notes   95
For Further Reading   97
Works Consulted   99
Works Cited   101
Index   106
Picture Credits   110
About the Author   111

Foreword

Each year on the first day of school, nearly every history teacher faces the task of explaining why his or her students should study history. One logical answer to this question is that exploring what happened in our past explains how the things we often take for granted—our customs, ideas, and institutions—came to be. As statesman and historian Winston Churchill put it, "Every nation or group of nations has its own tale to tell. Knowledge of the trials and struggles is necessary to all who would comprehend the problems, perils, challenges, and opportunities which confront us today." Thus, a study of history puts modern ideas and institutions in perspective. For example, though the founders of the United States were talented and creative thinkers, they clearly did not invent the concept of democracy. Instead, they adapted some democratic ideas that had originated in ancient Greece and with which the Romans, the British, and others had experimented. An exploration of these cultures, then, reveals their very real connection to us through institutions that continue to shape our daily lives.

Another reason often given for studying history is the idea that lessons exist in the past from which contemporary societies can benefit and learn. This idea, although controversial, has always been an intriguing one for historians. Those that agree that society can benefit from the past often quote philosopher George Santayana's famous statement, "Those who cannot remember the past are condemned to repeat it." Historians who ascribe to Santayana's philosophy believe that, for

example, studying the events that led up to the major world wars or other significant historical events would allow society to chart a different and more favorable course in the future.

Just as difficult as convincing students to realize the importance of studying history is the search for useful and interesting supplementary materials that present historical events in a context that can be easily understood. The volumes in Lucent Books' World History Series attempt to present a broad, balanced, and penetrating view of the march of history. Ancient Egypt's important wars and rulers, for example, are presented against the rich and colorful backdrop of Egyptian religious, social, and cultural developments. The series engages the reader by enhancing historical events with these cultural contexts. For example, in *Ancient Greece*, the text covers the role of women in that society. Slavery is discussed in *The Roman Empire*, as well as how slaves earned their freedom. The numerous and varied aspects of everyday life in these and other societies are explored in each volume of the series. Additionally, the series covers the major political, cultural, and philosophical ideas as the torch of civilization is passed from ancient Mesopotamia and Egypt, through Greece, Rome, Medieval Europe, and other world cultures, to the modern day.

The material in the series is formatted in a thorough, precise, and organized manner. Each volume offers the reader a comprehensive and clearly written overview of an important historical event or period. The topic under discussion is placed in a broad historical context. For example, *The Italian Renaissance* begins with a discussion of the High Middle Ages and the loss of central control that allowed certain Italian cities to develop artistically. The book ends by looking forward to the Reformation and interpreting the societal changes that grew out of the Renaissance. Thus, students are not only involved in an historical era, but also enveloped by the events leading up to that era and the events following it.

One important and unique feature in the World History Series is the primary and secondary source quotations that richly supplement each volume. These quotes are useful in a number of ways. First, they allow students access to sources they would not normally be exposed to because of the difficulty and obscurity of the original source. The quotations range from interesting anecdotes to farsighted cultural perspectives and are drawn from historical witnesses both past and present. Second, the quotes demonstrate how and where historians themselves derive their information on the past as they strive to reach a consensus on historical events. Lastly, all of the quotes are footnoted, familiarizing students with the citation process and allowing them to verify quotes and/or look up the original source if the quote piques their interest.

Finally, the books in the World History Series provide a detailed launching point for further research. Each book contains a bibliography specifically geared toward student research. A second, annotated bibliography introduces students to all the sources the author consulted when compiling the book. A chronology of important dates gives students an overview, at a glance, of the topic covered. Where applicable, a glossary of terms is included.

In short, the series is designed not only to acquaint readers with the basics of history, but also to make them aware that their lives are a part of an ongoing human saga. Perhaps they will then come to the same realization as famed historian Arnold Toynbee. In his monumental work, *A Study of History*, he wrote about becoming aware of history flowing through him in a mighty current, and of his own life "welling like a wave in the flow of this vast tide."

Important Dates in the History of the Italian Renaissance

1000	1050	1100	1150	1200	1250	1300

1000–1200
Independent, powerful city-states emerge in Italy

1095
Pope Urban II calls on Christians to participate in First Crusade

1209
Catholic Church begins crusade against the Albigensians

1210
Pope Innocent III recognizes Order of St. Francis

1300
Italians dominate commerce from London to Constantinople

ca. 1300–1350
Italians establish banking houses in Bruges, Paris, and London

1311
Papal court moves to Avignon, France

1348
Plague strikes Italy and all of Europe; Italy loses 35 to 50 percent of its population

1377
Pope Gregory XI returns the papacy to Rome

1378
Ciompi Revolt in Florence

1378–1417
Great Schism splits the Roman Catholic Church and Europe

1397
Medici Bank is founded; Manuel Chrysoloras comes to Florence

1417
Martin V becomes pope

1420
Construction of cathedral dome in Florence begins; Martin V returns an undivided papacy to Rome

1431
Eugenius IV becomes pope

1434
Cosimo de' Medici establishes rule in Florence; Pope Eugenius IV flees Rome

1436
Cosimo de' Medici finances Italy's first public library

1447
Nicholas V becomes pope

1450
Sforza family comes to power in Milan

1452
Leonardo da Vinci born

1453
The fall of Constantinople

1454
Venice and Milan negotiate Peace of Lodi; Italian League formed

1455
Calixtus III becomes pope

1458
Pius II becomes pope

1464
Paul II becomes pope

1469
Lorenzo de' Medici gains unofficial control of Florence

| 1350 | 1400 | 1450 | 1500 | 1550 | 1563 |

1471
Sixtus IV becomes pope

1475
Michelangelo Buonarroti born

ca. 1480
Florence under the one-man rule of Lorenzo de' Medici is no longer a republic

1483
Raphael Santi born

1484
Innocent VIII becomes pope

1492
Lorenzo de' Medici dies; Alexander VI becomes pope

1494
Charles VIII of France invades Italy and expels the Medici; Savonarola comes to power in Florence

1498
Savonarola executed

1499
Louis XII of France invades Italy

1503
Pius III becomes pope; Julius II becomes pope

1508
Ludovico Sforza dies in French captivity

1513
Machiavelli writes *The Prince*; Leo X becomes pope

1515
Francis I of France invades Italy

1517
Martin Luther posts his Ninety-five Theses in Wittenberg

1519
Charles V becomes Holy Roman Emperor

1521
Martin Luther excommunicated from Catholic Church

1522
Adrian VI becomes pope

1523
Clement VII becomes pope

1527
The sack of Rome

1534
Paul III becomes pope

1545
First meeting of Council of Trent

1546
Martin Luther dies

1562
Council of Trent meets for the last time

1563
Council of Trent ends

A Bridge in Time

When most people think of the Renaissance, they think of Michelangelo's Sistine Chapel, Leonardo da Vinci's *Mona Lisa,* and a myriad of other paintings, sculptures, and grand buildings that were created in Italy in the late fifteenth and early sixteenth centuries. Though these great artists and their works do, indeed, represent the era at its height, the Renaissance was more than an artistic revolution. Spanning several centuries (from roughly 1375 to 1625) all aspects of human life in Eu-

One of Michelangelo's greatest achievements is the stunning array of frescoes that adorn the Sistine Chapel. This fresco shows God creating the sun, moon, and planets. Though the Renaissance affected more than the artists, such masterpieces represent the era at its height.

rope underwent dramatic change. From the way people did business to how they conducted their politics to the way they built their homes, Renaissance men and women saw the new replace the old at a rapid pace.

The impulse for change began in Italy and for about a century (roughly 1375 to 1475) the Renaissance was a completely Italian phenomenon. Located at the crossroads between northern Europe, Africa, and Asia, Italy became a melting pot for ideas from vastly different cultures. From northern Europe, especially France, the Italians borrowed literary and musical styles which they adapted to their own tastes. From the East the Italians came into contact with a culture that was much more sophisticated than the one developing in Europe. The Arabs had a unique visual art style, which the Italians adapted and combined with the northern European style to create paintings, sculptures, and architectural works that were distinctly Italian. Arab scholars were far more advanced than their Western neighbors and from them the Italians learned much about astronomy, geography, medicine, and mathematics. As a result of this influx of ideas the cultural atmosphere in Italy was vibrant and conducive to experimentation and change—characteristics that influenced and attracted some of the most brilliant artists and scholars of the time. During the early Renaissance many of the most innovative thinkers and creative sculptors, painters, and architects were either born in Italy or drawn there by opportunities to learn, teach, practice their professions, and make their fortunes.

Because of its location Italy also emerged as a center of wealth during the late Middle Ages and early Renaissance.

Situated between East and West, the peninsula became a hub of trade. Such luxury goods as silk, spices, ivory, and pearls poured in from the East and were sold to northern Europeans by Italian merchant-bankers, who grew richer as the Renaissance progressed. In addition, the Italians developed local industries such as cloth manufacturing, which brought still more wealth to the peninsula.

Though most of the money made by Italy's merchants and bankers was reinvested in trade and industry, some of it was used to finance artists and scholars. During the Renaissance it became a matter of civic and personal pride to support artists and commission great works of art and architecture for the aggrandizement of the individual families and the glory of the cities in which they lived. Many wealthy families such as the Medici in Florence also supported writers and scholars who advocated social and cultural change.

Humanism

The most prominent strain of thought promoted by Renaissance scholars was humanism. Humanism was an educational program of study and a philosophical outlook that focused on the individual and his or her responsibilities to self and to community. Humanists taught that it was the duty of every person to strive for excellence and individuality in everything he or she did. Even more importantly, many humanists claimed that individuals were mandated by God to be the best they could be. For example, Giovanni Pico della Mirandola, one of the most famous Renaissance scholars, in his "Oration on the Dignity of Man," has God say to Adam: "With freedom of choice and with honor . . . thou mayest fashion thyself in whatever shape thou shalt prefer."[1] This mandate applied to all areas of human life. In education, politics, business, art, and craft, people were taught it was their duty to excel.

Humanists also instilled in Italians a pride in their past, claiming that Italy, the center of the Roman and Greek empires, was the birthplace of western European civilization and culture. Italian artists and

Pallas and the Centaur by Sandro Botticelli reflects the trend by Italian artists to incorporate mythological themes into their works.

scholars became preoccupied with ancient Greek and Roman writings, philosophy, and art, which they held to be a standard of excellence—a standard they believed had been all but extinguished during the Middle Ages. By resurrecting the ancient methods and teachings, Renaissance scholars thought they were restoring civilization and high culture to Europe. In 1492, Marsilio Ficino wrote: "Achieving what had been honored among the ancients, but almost forgotten since, [this] age has . . . recalled teaching from darkness to light."[2]

In the nineteenth century Swiss historian Jacob Burckhardt adopted roughly this same view, defining the Renaissance as a time of innovation, human self-discovery, artistic excellence, and cultural change, which represented a complete break with western Europe's medieval past and the beginning of modern European culture.

Though the term Renaissance is still used to describe the period between 1375 and 1625, most modern scholars do not see the Middle Ages as having been so dark nor the changes as having been so abrupt. Today, the Renaissance is seen as the natural product of a progression of social, political, cultural, and economic changes rooted in earlier times and evolving over several centuries. Rather than a single event or a compressed series of events, the Renaissance is considered by many to be a bridge in time, in which one event or impulse led to another and spanned the centuries between the Middle Ages and the birth of modern Europe. The story of the Renaissance is the history of that evolution.

Chapter

1 The Seeds of the Italian Renaissance

The seeds of the Renaissance first sprouted in Italy. This in part was due to Italy's prime location as an international trading center. Situated on the southern tip of Europe and thrusting into the Mediterranean Sea, Italy was surrounded on three sides by navigable waters. The Mediterranean lay to the south, the Adriatic to the east, and the Tyrrhenian to the west. These waterways allowed Italy to act as a trade link between northern Europe and the rich and mysterious East.

As early as the tenth and eleventh centuries, individual cities in Italy were evolving into city-states. City-states were established commercial centers that, by virtue of some geographical, trade, or agricultural advantage, grew and incorporated surrounding rural and urban areas. Thus, during most of the Middle Ages Italy was not a unified country but rather a group of independent territories, each with its own form of government. For example, in the south the kingdom of Naples was ruled by non-Italian monarchs. The Papal States, to the north of Naples, were under the control of a succession of popes, the titular heads of the Catholic Church. Milan, in the north, was dominated by the one-man rule of a series of dukes. And in northern and central Italy, embryonic city-states such as Florence and Venice were forming republican governments in which select people elected their own governing councils. Otto of Freising, a twelfth-century writer, described the emerging city-states in northern Italy:

> They are so attached to their liberty that, to avoid the insolence of rulers, they prefer to be reigned over by con-

RENAISSANCE ITALY

SAVOY
Turin
MONTFERRAT
Milan
MILAN
Mantua
Padua
Venice
REPUBLIC OF VENICE
Parma
PARMA
MANTUA
Modena
MODENA
Genoa
FIVIZANNO
MASSA
LUCCA
Florence
Pisa
FLORENCE
REPUBLIC OF GENOA
PAPAL STATES
Adriatic Sea
PIOMBINO
Rome
NAPLES
Mediterranean Sea
Naples
SARDINIA

Italian city-states relied on foreign trade for their economic survival. Traders headed east from thriving Italian ports such as Venice.

suls than by princes. . . . Lest they [the consuls] should be seized with a greed for power, they are changed nearly every year.[3]

The strength of many emerging city-states was based on their ability to conduct foreign trade. From the ports of Venice in the northeast, Genoa and Pisa in the northwest, and Naples and Amalfi in the south, ships sailed for the East, heading for the northern coast of Africa, where the Italians purchased gold, and for cities along the eastern coast for the Mediterranean, which were outlets for luxury goods from the Far East. In Constantino-

ple, Antioch, Beirut, Tyre, Acre, and other eastern cities, Italian merchants could purchase silks, spices, camphor, musk, pearls, and ivory brought from as far away as India and China.

These luxury goods were in high demand in the markets of northern Europe. Sailing west, then north, Italian ships traveled to Spain, the Netherlands, and the British Isles to sell their cargoes to rich kings, the nobility, or other merchants. Goods were also transported overland from the Italian peninsula to Germany and France for sale.

On return trips from England and Flanders, a medieval county in northwest Europe, Italian traders imported raw wool and cloth, stimulating a growing Italian textile industry. In the following centuries

A wealthy fifteenth-century Italian merchant inspects goods at a port. Through foreign trade, Italians were exposed to a wealth of ideas from diverse cultures.

The textile industry flourished in Italy after Italian traders imported wool and cloth.

Italian artisans, especially those in Florence, perfected techniques for dyeing, weaving, and finishing wool that would become the finest on three continents and bring vast wealth to Italy.

A Wealth of Ideas

Long-distance trade affected other than mercantile aspects of Italian culture, exposing Italians to the arts and sciences of many diverse cultures. From the East, for example, Italian artists were influenced by Byzantine artists who, to a large extent, worked with tile and made mosaics. Their creations were characterized by bold lines,

geometrical arrangements of figures, and an absence of visual depth. Eventually Byzantine masters taught in Italian academies and decorated churches in major cities, such as St. Agnes's in Rome, and St. Mark's in Venice.

From the East the Italians also came into contact with cultures that had more advanced systems of science and philosophy. Historian De Lamar Jensen writes:

> In science and philosophy, the Arabs had no peers. They made great strides in astronomy, geography, medicine, and mathematics, especially algebra and trigonometry, and adopted the indispensable "Arabic" numerals from India and introduced them to the West. They translated and studied Aristotle and other Greek philosophers as well as their own, and made available commentaries of expert Spanish-Arab scholars.[4]

Other ideas and styles reached Italy from France, which was then the cultural center of Europe. Italian artists, musicians, and traders brought back the art and ideas of northern Europe; important among these were the songs and literature of courtly love. As in the following stanzas by an anonymous poet, such verse characteristically paid tribute to a perfect and unattainable lady:

> I sing of her, yet her beauty
> is greater than I can tell,
> with her fresh color, lively eyes,
> and white skin, untanned
> and untainted by rouge.
> She is so pure and noble
> that no one can speak ill of her.
> But above all, one must praise,
> it seems to me, her truthfulness,

Thirteenth-century poet Dante Alighieri wrote epic love sonnets that included the theme of courtly love.

her manners and her gracious speech for she never would betray a friend.[5]

The theme of courtly love would provide subject matter for Italian poets for centuries to come. Among the masterpieces of both thirteenth-century poet Dante Alighieri and fourteenth-century writer Francesco Petrarch are poems written to their unattainable loves, Beatrice and Laura.

More important than subject matter was the fact that French songs and poems were often written in the spoken language of the average person, not in Latin, the language of the church and intellectual elite. This prompted Italians to write in the languages (of which there were many) of their people and to develop a popular literature of their own.

The Crusades

In the eleventh, twelfth, and thirteenth centuries the multicultural links between East and West forged by trade were strengthened by military means. In the preceding centuries, Eastern cities considered holy by Christians, such as Jerusalem and Bethlehem, had come under Muslim control. From 1096 to 1291 soldiers fought a series of "holy wars" known as the Crusades to secure these cities in the East against Muslim rule. James A. Brundage writes:

> The very fact that these Holy Places were ruled by and frequented by non-Christians was considered wicked and abominable by most European Christians, for it constituted, they believed, a crime in the sight of God.[6]

Hundreds of thousands of European Christians responded to civil and religious authorities' calls to arms, and many of these crusaders left for the Middle East via Italy, especially Venice, where they could hire ships and buy provisions for their journey. Their purchases added huge sums to the coffers of Italy, further strengthening the Italian economy.

More importantly, the crusaders helped Italy establish trade centers in the East. Quite often, if the crusaders lacked money to pay for provisions, traders and other rich, powerful Italians would provide money and needed goods in exchange for the rights to establish exclusive trading quarters in the cities the crusaders conquered. These districts would include markets, docks, and churches, all of which were controlled by the city that had sponsored the soldiers. For example, Venice operated a center in Jerusalem, as did

Genoa in Tripoli. The Italians, with permanent trading bases along the Mediterranean, virtually controlled the sea trade.

The Bankers of Europe

Expanding trade created an increasing need for innovative banking and business practices. In order to finance costly long-distance voyages, the Italians developed systems of credit that allowed merchants to borrow, loan, and pool money to finance commercial ventures. They adopted better bookkeeping techniques and were better able to cultivate new markets for their goods. They also developed a system

enabling traders to purchase insurance against the loss of or damage to their ships and cargoes.

By 1300 the Italians dominated commerce from London to Constantinople. By the middle of the century, they operated banking houses in Bruges, Paris, and London. They financed business ventures and loaned money to the popes in Rome and to the monarchs of Europe. Interest collected on these loans poured into Italian city-states, whose wealth grew. Their ability to finance anything from voyages of exploration to wars made increasingly powerful Italian bankers major players in the politics of northern Europe.

Because the Italians tended to limit partnerships to their kin, rich banking

The Crusades were a series of religious wars designed to rid the world of Muslims. Crusaders bought provisions and hired ships in Italy, contributing to its thriving economy.

families emerged at this time. In Florence the Bardi, Peruzzi, and Acciaiuoli families amassed great fortunes. In Lucca, so did the Ricciardi. The rise of these families was another medieval precondition setting the stage for the Renaissance. They were "new men" with power and money, and their needs charted Italy's social, cultural, political, and economic course. Their rise to power changed the social order of Italy.

Most of Europe in the Middle Ages was a feudal society, comprising three basic classes—the clergy, the landed nobility, and laborers. Laborers included both ur-ban artisans, who were skilled craftsmen, and rural peasants who tilled the soil. By the middle of the eleventh century, how-ever, merchants and long-distance traders formed a fourth group, which by the twelfth century included bankers. In Italy, especially, these men were able to chal-lenge the traditional landed nobility. The new urban rich gained power through po-litical maneuvering in city governments, open warfare with the nobility, and through arranged marriages. Marriages between the old rich and the new rich pro-vided a way for the two classes to resolve

The City of Venice

In the middle of the thirteenth century, Venice was a bustling center of trade. In Henry Hart's book Marco Polo: Venetian Adventurer, *Martino da Canale, a thirteenth-century historian, describes the port city.*

"Venice, today [is] the most beautiful and the pleasantest city in all the world, full of beauty and of all good things. Merchandise flows through this noble city even as the water flows from the fountains. Venice is enthroned upon the sea, and the salt water flows through it and about it and in all places, save in the houses and on the streets, and when the citizens go forth, they can return to their homes either by sea or by the streets. From every place come merchandise and merchants, who buy the merchandise as they will and cause it to be taken to their own countries. Within this city is found food in great abundance, bread and wine, chickens and river fowls, meat, both fresh and salt, the great fish both of the sea and of the rivers, and merchants of every country who sell and buy. You may find in plenty within this beautiful city men of good breeding, old and middle-aged and young, much to be praised for their noble character, and merchants who sell and buy, and money changers and citizens of every craft, and seafaring men of every sort, and vessels to carry [goods] to every port, and galleys to destroy their enemies."

A potter spins clay on a wheel, crafting a vessel with a variety of uses. During the Middle Ages, laborers, including skilled craftsmen, comprised a large social class.

their differences peacefully. Historians write:

> Marriage vows often sealed business contracts between the rural nobility and the mercantile aristocracy. This merger of the northern Italian feudal nobility and the commercial aristocracy constituted the formation of a new social class, an urban nobility.[7]

As this urban nobility gained status, money—not noble birth—became the criteria for power, as this work by thirteenth-century poet Cecco Angiolieri illustrates:

> Preach what you will,
> Florins [gold coins] are the best of kin:
> Blood brothers and cousins true,
> Father, mother, sons, and daughters too;
> Kinfolk of the sort no one regrets,
> Also horses, mules, and beautiful dress.
> The French and the Italians bow to them,
> So do noblemen, knights, and learned men.
> Florins clear your eyes and give you fires,
> Turn to facts all your desires
> And into all the world's vast possibilities.
> So no man say, I'm nobly born, if
> He have not money. Let him say,
> I was born like a mushroom, in obscurity and wind.[8]

Wealthy and powerful, the descendants of these bankers and merchants would choose to display their accomplishments in forms more dramatic than account book tallies. Their pride would manifest itself through art and culture. They would sponsor artists, musicians, writers, and philosophers to promote the glory of their families and their city-states, to which they were intensely loyal.

The Roman Catholic Church

As loyalty to the secular city-states rose, and bankers and merchants gained power, the focus of medieval life in Italy shifted. Traders and bankers influenced public policy in areas that formerly were primarily the domain of the church, prompting a change in institutionalized education. During much of the Middle Ages, the church held a virtual monopoly on education, reserving it for the clergy. But in the late

During much of the Middle Ages, priests (pictured) and other members of the clergy were among the few that attained an education. This changed in the late twelfth century when the proliferation of trade created a need for secretaries and notaries.

twelfth century the rise in trade created a demand for secretaries and notaries. By the thirteenth century, nonreligious vocational schools were training students for jobs in government and trade.

The admission of lay students in the elementary schools and universities and the development of a secular curriculum offered a wider variety of educational experiences to a larger number of people. This loosened the church's control over learning and paved the way for other secular educational programs that would typify the Renaissance.

In the late twelfth century, the church was also losing power and influence due to its increased secularization. By the tenth century, the church was the largest landowner in western Europe. With wealth had come power. By the thirteenth century, in places as far away from Rome as England and France, Catholic popes had the ability to appoint church officials and collect taxes from foreign parishes. They also intrigued in the politics of Italy and northern Europe, supporting various factions and leaders against one another.

The pursuit of wealth undermined the church's popular support. As early as the late twelfth century, people throughout Europe criticized its materialism. Disillusioned, some joined cult religions that sought to reform or overthrow the Catholic Church. Two of the most influential groups, the Waldensians and the Albigensians, originated in France and spread to northern Italy in the late twelfth and early thirteenth centuries. The Waldensians objected to the moral laxity and wealth of the clergy. The Albigensians preached against the priesthood, claiming the Catholic Church had been corrupted by worldliness. Members of the two groups were denounced as heretics by Pope Innocent III, who launched a crusade against the Albigensians in 1209. For two decades southern France was the scene of a bloody eradication of the Albigensians by the church.

Even those who remained loyal to the church worked toward reform. The Italian friar Francis of Assisi, canonized in 1228, protested against the materialism of the church and advocated poverty for his followers. In the early thirteenth century, he wrote:

> The brothers shall appropriate nothing to themselves, neither a house, nor a place, nor anything; but as pilgrims and strangers in this world, in poverty

and humility serving God, they shall confidently go seeking for alms.[9]

The Avignon Papacy and the Great Schism

Even people who were not involved in religious reform movements also began to question the role of the pope. In the early fourteenth century, Pope Boniface VIII struggled with King Philip IV of France for political power. The pope wanted church authority over that of the secular rulers of Europe, including France; and Philip wanted a degree of control over the clergy in his country. For example, Philip wanted the right to tax the rich French

clergy without seeking the consent of the pope. There was much political maneuvering, and even open hostility. In 1303, the French launched an attack on Boniface and attempted, but failed, to execute him. Boniface died a few months later, and was replaced by Benedict XI, who lived only a few months.

Benedict was succeeded by Clement V, who, in 1311, gave in to French demands and moved the papal court from Rome to France, beginning what is known as the Avignon Papacy. For sixty-six years the next six popes resided at Avignon. Then in 1377 Pope Gregory XI moved the papacy back to Rome, succeeded at his death the following year by Urban VI.

Distressed by the move and not wanting to lose the prestige of having the pa-

A Pope's Call to Arms

During the Middle Ages European soldiers participated in the Crusades. In The First Crusade: The Chronicle of Fulcher of Chartres and Other Source Material, *Robert the Monk summarizes a call to arms he heard delivered by Pope Urban II on November 26, 1095.*

"Jerusalem is the navel of the world; the land is fruitful above others, like another paradise of delights. This the Redeemer of the human race has made illustrious by His advent, has beautified by residence, has consecrated by suffering, has redeemed by death, has glorified by burial. This royal city, therefore, situated at the centre of the world, is now held captive by His enemies, and is in subjection to those who do not know God, to the worship of the heathens. She seeks therefore and desires to be liberated, and does not cease to implore you to come to her aid. From you especially she asks succor, because, as we have already said, God has conferred upon you above all nations great glory in arms. Accordingly undertake this journey for the remission of your sins, with the assurance of the imperishable glory of the kingdom of heaven."

pal court in France, the French king, Charles V, supported the election of his cousin as a second pope, Clement VII. For the next forty years two popes (and at one time, three) claimed papal authority in Europe. England, much of Germany, northern and central Italy, Flanders, and Ireland supported Urban. France, Naples, Sicily, Spain, Portugal, and Scotland supported Clement. The Great Schism, as it was called, divided Europe and severely damaged the papacy and the church. The popes were humiliated and their power was weakened by their political losses to the monarchs of France. As the church fell into confusion, the monarchs of northern Europe and the merchant class in Italy gained more control over cultural and political developments in their regions. This confusion, com-

The bubonic plague swept through Europe and Asia between 1347 and 1351, leaving a devastating trail of sickness and death. The resulting decline in population had far-reaching economic effects.

Giotto di Bondone

"A crude fellow had heard of his [Giotto's] renown, and since he needed to have his shield painted . . . immediately went to Giotto's workshop . . . where he found Giotto, he said: 'God save you, Master. I would like you to paint my arms on this shield.' Sizing up the man and his manners, Giotto said nothing but 'When do you want it?' . . . When Giotto was alone, he thought to himself: 'What does this mean . . . asking me to paint his coat of arms as if he were from the royal house of France. I'll certainly make him an unusual coat of arms.'

And so thinking this over, Giotto . . . designed something he thought appropriate. . . . The painting showed a small helmet, a gorget [throat armor], a pair of armlets, a pair of iron gloves, a pair of cuirasses [back and breast armor] and greaves [leg armor], a sword, a knife, and a lance. When the worthy man . . . returned, he . . . enquired: 'Master, is my shield painted?'. . . When the shield arrived, this would-be gentleman . . . said to Giotto: 'What's this mess you've daubed on it?'. . . Giotto said: 'What did you tell me to paint?' And the man answered: 'My arms.' Giotto said: 'And aren't they all here?'"

bined with changes in education and a push for reform, resulted in an increasingly secular society, another hallmark of the Renaissance.

The Rise of the Middle Class

The church was also weakened by the bubonic plague, which devastated Europe between 1347 and 1351. In Germany alone the church lost one-third of its clergy. Preceded by famine, the Black Death, as it was called, spread from the East to the ports of Italy and up through Europe. Giovanni Boccaccio described the spread of the 1348 plague:

> The death-dealing pestilence . . . had some years before appeared in the parts of the East and after having bereft these latter of an innumerable number of inhabitants, extending without cease from one place to an-

other, had now unhappily spread toward the West.[10]

Though there had been plagues before and many would follow, none had been or would be more deadly. It is estimated that Europe lost two-fifths of its population between 1348 and 1350. Italy lost 35 to 50 percent of its people: The population of Florence fell from 80,000 to 30,000, of Pistoia from 24,000 to 14,000, and Siena lost half its citizens.

The abrupt decline in population had far-reaching implications for the Italians. The traditional nobility, whose wealth was in vast landholdings, lost power. The plague meant fewer people to feed and prices for agricultural goods fell dramatically. At the same time, there were fewer peasants, members of the rural working class, to till the soil. Many died of the plague or moved to cities where jobs, left vacant by the deaths of skilled artisans, opened up. Peasants who stayed in the country could, because of the decline in the labor force, demand higher wages at a time when landlords could not afford it.

The Italian urban working class, made up of such skilled artisans as bakers, candle makers, apothecaries, and weavers, benefited from the plague if they survived it. Because of their decreased numbers and increased demand for their labor, they could command higher prices for the products they made and insist on better working conditions. Trade guilds, associations of artisans, wielded greater power in the government of the city-states. Historian Donald Kagan writes: "The merchant and patrician classes found it increasingly difficult to maintain their traditional dominance and grudgingly gave guild masters a voice in city government."[11] More and more the newly powerful urban working class aligned itself with merchants and bankers against the traditional nobility, building a strong middle class in Italy.

The rise of the merchant and middle classes, combined with diminished church authority, set the stage for the Renaissance in Italy. With the old order crumbling and a new one gaining strength, the Italian culture changed steadily. Synthesizing the old with the new became the preoccupation of Italy's scholars, artists, and urban aristocracy. As they worked to reconcile tradition with innovation, they ushered in the Renaissance.

2 The Early Renaissance in Florence

The Renaissance began in Florence, a thriving city-state in northern Italy. From the middle of the fourteenth century until the early sixteenth century, Florence was a dynamic and creative center of art and learning. In painting, sculpture, and architecture, the Florentines excelled. Most of the prominent artists of the day were either born in Florence or did their best work there: Among others, the architect Brunelleschi, the painter Masaccio, and the sculptor Donatello created works of lasting importance that would become hallmarks of the early Renaissance.

Florentine scholars also made significant contributions to the disciplines of history, literature, moral philosophy, law, theology, and medicine. Giovanni Boccaccio, who wrote both popular and scholarly literature, was the son of a Florentine businessman and lived much of his life in that city. Leonardo Bruni, a scholar, historian, and teacher, was Florentine, as was Leon Battista Alberti, an architect who wrote treatises on the art and architecture of the period. One of the greatest musicians of the day, composer Guillaume Dufay, worked in Florence. With a wealth of native talent augmented by the influx of still more, the city rapidly became a focal point of cultural activity.

Why the rebirth began in Florence and why much of the innovation of the early Renaissance took place there is, in many ways, a mystery. As historian James Cleugh writes:

> Florence, even in her most glorious days in the fifteenth and sixteenth centuries, was never the first city of Italy, and she possessed no extraordinary advantages, natural or otherwise. To the contrary, of the six major political divisions in Italy at the end of the Middles Ages, she seemed the least endowed. The kingdoms of Sicily and Naples enjoyed a far richer cultural and intellectual heritage. Rome, fortified by an imperial tradition and sustained by a series of ambitious and powerful popes, had long claimed, and sometimes realized, the hegemony [dominance] not only of Italy but of all of Europe. Venice and Milan both possessed greater political and military power. Yet it was in Florence, rather than in any of her more obviously blessed sisters, that the glory of the Renaissance was to germinate and come to fruition.[12]

The Florentines were able to make up for what they lacked in some areas by exploiting their city's advantages. Unlike many other rich city-states, Florence was

The Pride of Florence

During the early Renaissance Florence was a thriving city-state, and its citizens took great pride in all that concerned it. In a letter written in 1472 and quoted in Gertrude R. B. Richards's Florentine Merchants in the Age of the Medici, *Florentine Benedetto Dei brags about his city, and exaggerates its good points.*

"Florence is more beautiful and five hundred forty years older than your Venice. . . . We have round about us thirty thousand estates, owned by noblemen and merchants, citizens and craftsmen, yielding us yearly bread and meat, wine and oil, vegetables and cheese, hay and wood. . . . We have two trades greater than any four of yours in Venice put together—the trades of wool and silk. Witness the Roman court and that of the King of Naples . . . and Sicily, where, to your envy and disgust, in all of those places there are Florentine consuls and merchants, churches and houses, banks and offices, and whither go more Florentine wares of all kinds, especially silken stuffs and gold and silver brocades, than from Venice, Genoa and Lucca put together. Ask your merchants . . . where there are great banks and royal warehouses, fine dwellings, and stately churches; ask those who should know . . . whether they have seen the banks of the Medici, the Pazzi, the Capponi, the Buondelmonti, the Corsini, the Falconieri, the Portinari, and the Ghini, and a hundred of others which I will not name, because to do so I should need at least a ream of paper."

The Renaissance took firm hold in Florence, a thriving city-state in northern Italy.

not a seaport. Situated about fifty miles from the Mediterranean Sea along the Arno River in a hilly region called Tuscany, Florence instead enjoyed the many benefits of access to a freshwater resource. The Arno supplied Florence with a constant supply of drinking water, which was often in short supply in inland cities such as Siena, Perugia, and Cortona. Fish from the Arno was an important part of the Florentine diet and flour mills powered by the river ground meal for bread, another staple. Sanitary conditions in Florence were also better than in such cities as Siena because of the proximity of the river.

The Arno also played a major role in Florence's textile industry. Washing, fulling (shrinking and thickening), and dyeing cloth required a constant supply of fresh water, which the river provided. By the middle of the fourteenth century almost one-third of the hundred thousand people living in Florence worked making cloth. Spinners, weavers, dyers, merchants, and shopkeepers, among other specialists, composed an industry that brought the city the equivalent of nearly $5 million a year.

The Arno gave merchants access to markets for their wares, as well. Downstream, it linked Florence with the prospering city-state of Pisa and the sea, whose trade routes led to northern Europe. Upstream, the Florentines could travel to the city of Arezzo, another important urban center, which was a stop on the way to Rome.

Along with the Arno, the Tuscan terrain offered Florentines more geographical advantages. Major roads linked Florence to Milan, Venice, Bologna, Perugia, and Assisi, all important Italian urban centers. An eastern route over the Apennine Mountains to the Adriatic Sea gave Florentines access to the East, where they could sell their finished cloth and purchase such necessary raw materials as dye.

Because Florence enjoyed a higher elevation and greater distance from valley marshes than other river cities, it was not plagued by malaria and the swamp diseases that devastated cities such as Pisa. The Tuscan countryside also helped provide the city a stable food supply. Olive oil, wine, and, to a lesser degree, grain from Tuscan farms fed some of Florence's urban populace.

Merchants and Bankers

As successful businessmen, Florentine bankers and merchants had by this time outstripped their rivals in other cities. At the end of the thirteenth century, Florentine bankers had gained control of papal banking and tax collecting. This brought them a share of church profits, which they used to establish a monopoly on international banking and trade. From London to Paris, from Barcelona to Tunis, Florentine merchants sold their goods, invested their money, and brought their profits back to Florence. They also exploited Naples to the south, holding a monopoly on the region's grain trade.

The Arno River and the Tuscan countryside thus provided the basic necessities of food, water, sanitation, and transportation. The textile industry provided jobs and a strong economic base. Florentine merchants and bankers multiplied the city's wealth, which was used to strengthen Florence's economic dominance in

In the fifteenth century, the Medici in Florence rose to prominence as one of the richest and most distinguished families in Europe. Banking was one lucrative source of Medici wealth.

northern Italy. These advantages would sustain the Florentine people and their economy through the political, social, and economic crises that periodically struck Florence, and all of Italy, throughout the early Renaissance.

Another factor that contributed to the cultural growth and stability of Florence was the presence of one of the richest families in Europe—the Medici.

The House of Medici

Cosimo de' Medici brought his family to prominence in Florence in the early fifteenth century. In the 1430s the Medici was the third richest family in the city. In 1434, the family came to political power when members of the Albizzi family, the Medici's archrivals, were exiled. By 1457, under the direction of Cosimo, the Medici

family was both the wealthiest and most powerful in all of Florence.

Medici money came from diverse sources. Originally they amassed a fortune from a bank founded by Cosimo's father in 1397. By 1451 this bank had expanded and the family operated seven branches in cities outside of Florence, including London, Lyon, and Antwerp. The Medici also derived income from international trade and owned two wool shops and a silk shop at home. Their growing wealth brought growing political power.

Cosimo was a behind-the-scenes ruler. He officially held the highest public office only three times during his life, for a total of only about six months. His real power came from unofficial manipulation of government appointments and the justice system. At that time, Florentine politics were based on an intricate network of patronage and favor trade-offs. Florence was divided into four districts, each of which was represented in the central government by two priors. These priors, along with the *gonfalonier,* their chairman, made up the Signori, the most important governing body. The Signori met with various less prestigious committees to issue or approve policies of importance to Florence in such areas as trade regulations, taxation, public improvements, and building construction.

There were many of these decision-making bodies, often comprising a large number of members. For example, the Council of the People and the Council of the Commune, two legislative bodies, combined had five hundred members. Every year more than three thousand government positions in Florence and the other cities they incorporated (such as Pisa, which came under Florentine control in 1406) fell vacant and needed to be filled.

The Medici learned to manipulate this system to their advantage. Because the Medici were so wealthy, they were in a position to loan money and grant both professional and personal favors to people who in turn owed the Medici social and political favors and voted the way the Medici wanted them to. Soon the Medici were recognized as the unofficial rulers of Florence.

They were also recognized as leaders outside of the city-state. Because of their foreign banking and trade enterprises, the Medici had created friendships with some

---

Cosimo de' Medici

Cosimo de' Medici brought his family to prominence in Florence in the early fifteenth century. Renaissance historian and political theorist Niccolo Machiavelli describes him in History of Florence.

"Cosmo [sic] de' Medici, after the death of Giovanni [his father], engaged more earnestly in public affairs, and conducted himself with more zeal and boldness in regard to his friends than his father had done. . . . Cosmo was one of the most prudent of men; of grave and courteous demeanor, extremely liberal and humane. He never attempted anything against parties, or against rulers, but was bountiful to all; and, by the unwearied generosity of his disposition, made himself partisans of all ranks of citizens. This mode of proceeding increased the difficulties of those who were in the government, and Cosmo himself hoped that by its pursuit he might be able to live in Florence as much respected and secure as any other citizen; or if the ambition of his adversaries compelled him to adopt a different course, arm and the favor of his friends would enable him to become more so."

of the most powerful people in both Europe and the East. They were the only family in Florence to have hosted visits from two emperors, Frederick III of Germany and John Paleologue of Byzantium, bringing both the family and their city added prestige. To outsiders they appeared to have the power of kings. Pope Pius II, after meeting Cosimo in 1459, wrote:

> He it is who decides the peace and war and controls the laws. . . . Political questions are settled at his house. The men he chooses hold office. He is a king in all but name and ceremony.[13]

Cosimo's clan had rivals, however. Other families, such as the Albizzi and the Pazzi, also wanted control of Florence. When power could not be obtained through peaceful political maneuvering or the exile of rivals, wealthy families sometimes resorted to violence, including murder and even public skirmishes in which the backers of the warring parties would meet in open conflict on the city streets. Luca Landucci, a Florentine apothecary, described the carnage that resulted after a member of the Pazzi family murdered a Medici:

> All the city was up in arms, in the Piazza and at Lorenzo de' Medici's house. And numbers of men on the side of the conspirators were killed in the Piazza; amongst others a priest of the bishop's was killed there, his body being quartered and the head cut off, and then the head was stuck on the top of a lance, and carried about Florence the whole day, and one quarter of his body was carried on a spit all the through, with a cry of: "Death to the traitors!"[14]

Business and politics were not the only occupations of the Medici. They were among the most avid patrons of art and scholarship in Florence. During Cosimo's lifetime the principal architects of the early Renaissance—Brunelleschi and Michelozzo, and the great sculptors Donatello and Ghiberti—were working in Florence. At some point in their careers all were under the patronage of the Medici. James Cleugh writes: "A practical result of this munificence [generous patronage] was that in these fields, what is generally known as 'Renaissance culture' began earlier in Florence than elsewhere."[15]

The Medici spent huge sums of money patronizing the arts. Benozzo Gozzoli's fresco Journey of the Magi *adorns the walls of a Medici chapel and features portraits of several Medici family members.*

The Medici also fostered scholarship. Cosimo's money financed searching out, editing, and preserving ancient Greek and Latin manuscripts to expand his library. In addition, he commissioned the first public library in Italy, built in 1436. Cosimo also helped finance the Florentine Platonic Academy, where some of the most brilliant scholars of the time met to discuss philosophy.

A powerful patron and politician, Cosimo solidified Medici prominence in Florence. His grandson Lorenzo, known as "the Magnificent," followed in his footsteps and became one of the strongest rulers in Florence's history.

Lorenzo the Magnificent

Lorenzo de' Medici's father, Piero, headed the family for only about five years. Sickly throughout most of his life, Piero died in 1469, leaving the care of Florence in the hands of his young son. Fortunately, Cosimo and Piero had groomed the young Lorenzo for his lofty position. Even before Piero's death, Lorenzo had been sent on diplomatic missions entrusted with the power to negotiate with popes and kings. He had been primed to assume control of the city. On the death of his father, Lorenzo later wrote:

> Although I, Lorenzo, was very young, being twenty years of age, the principal men of the city and of the regime came to us in our house to condole with us on our loss and to encourage me to take charge of the city and the regime as my grandfather and father had done. This I did, though on account of my youth and the great peril

Lorenzo the Magnificent was one of the most brilliant leaders of the Renaissance. Under his rule, the Medici strengthened their control over Florence.

and responsibility arising therefrom, with great reluctance, solely for the safety of our friends and of our possessions. For it is ill living in Florence for the rich unless they rule.[16]

Under Lorenzo, Florence was brought even more tightly under Medici control. By 1480 the city was no longer a republic, but was becoming an oligarchy, a governmental system in which a small, rich ruling class holds power. After Lorenzo took his father's place, constitutional changes were enacted that increased the power of the Medici and reduced the power of the people. Lorenzo created a new committee called the Council of Seventy, a group of handpicked men who served for life. From the time of its inception, the Council of Seventy controlled all aspects of Florentine politics, and the older, communal institutions declined in status and power. Lorenzo, a member of the Council of Seventy, had direct representation in its two most powerful committees—the Eight of War, and the Twelve of Finance and Commerce. Now, as quasi-official head of the city and its government, Lorenzo had substantial control over most important foreign and domestic decisions. As his power increased, Lorenzo assumed a status more of a prince than of a citizen of a republic.

While Lorenzo expanded Medici control over Florence, he also continued another family tradition as a patron of the arts. He loved beautiful things and surrounded himself with precious gems and antique art. Though artistic works he is known to have commissioned are few, he did employ some of the best artists in Florence. The painters Perugino and Botticelli and the fresco master Ghirlandaio all worked on projects for Lorenzo. His influence on the visual arts throughout Italy was strong, as historian Gene Brucker writes: "Lorenzo was recognized as the premier connoisseur of the arts in Italy, and his advice on painters and architects was sought by princes throughout the peninsula. . . . As one dimension of his foreign policy, he sent Florentine artists to

A Marriage Arrangement

In Renaissance Italy marriages were quite often arranged to consolidate the power and wealth of two families. In his diary, included in Two Memoirs of Renaissance Florence *edited by Gene Brucker, Buonaccorso Pitti, a businessman and professional gambler, described how he chose his bride.*

"On reaching Florence I resolved to get married. Since Guido di Messer Tommaso di Neri del Palagio was the most respected and influential man in the city, I decided to put the matter in his hands and leave the choice of bride up to him, provided he picked her among his own relatives. For I calculated that if I were to become a connection of his and could win his good will, he would be obliged to help me obtain a truce with the Corbizi family. Accordingly, I sent the marriage-broker, Bartolo della Contessa, to tell Guido of my intentions. He sent Bartolo back with the message that he would be happy to have me as kinsman and was giving the matter thought. A few days later he sent him a second time to say that if I liked I might have the daughter of Luca, son of Piero degli Albizzi, whose mother was a first cousin of his own. I sent back word that I would be very happy and honored and so forth. I was betrothed to her at the end of July 1391 and married her on 12 November of the same year."

The estate of the Medici reflects the great wealth of Florence's ruling family.

work for those rulers whose favor he desired."[17] The favor and patronage of Lorenzo, then, could greatly add to an artist's prestige and income. In this way Lorenzo's taste can be said to have affected Renaissance aesthetics.

Lorenzo also supported the writers and scholars of his day, offering them lodging and work in his household. Among others, the philosopher and teacher Marsilio Ficino, the scholar and writer Giovanni Pico della Mirandola and the poet Matteo Franco found employment in the Medici household. Lorenzo himself was a recognized poet of the Renaissance. Well educated and sensitive, he wrote verses that were ranked with the best of his age. In the following sonnet he looks at life and death:

> How fruitless is each human hope,
>   how vain
>   And false is every plan we may
>   conceive,
>   How full of ignorance the world,
>   believe—

Death, who is mistress of everything,
    makes plain.
Some live to sing, to joust, to dance
    again;
  Others for quiet pleasure all this will
    leave;
  Some scorn a worldly life whose lures
    deceive;
  Others show what's in their hearts
    disdain.
Vain cares and thoughts, men's diverse
    lot, the fate
  That nature gives in her variety,
  One sees each moment wandering
    the world over.
All that we see is fleeting, brief estate,
  So great on earth Fortune's inequity:
  Nothing but Death stands firm and
    lasts forever.[18]

Under the Medici, Florentine culture during the early Renaissance flourished. In education, scholarship, and the arts, Florence became Europe's focal point of cultural change.

3 Humanism in the Early Renaissance

In Italy, the Trecento—the 1300s—and the Quattrocento—the 1400s—were periods of dynamic cultural change and great advance in scholarship. New forms of literature and an entire philosophy appeared. Pioneers in education introduced their students to studies of literature, grammar, speech making, history, and writing based on that philosophy. Eloquent politicians, schooled in this new way, integrated education with politics to advance and refine the art of diplomacy and shape the governments of their city-states.

These developments in scholarship, education, and the political arts had their roots in humanism, a philosophy and program of study that swept Italy in the early Renaissance. As a philosophy humanism emphasized the central importance of humans and their work. Historian Marvin Perry writes:

> The humanists . . . made the achievement of excellence through individual striving the end not only of education but of life itself. Because individuals were capable of . . . [excellence] . . . it was their duty to pursue it.[19]

The pursuit of excellence, however, did not mean rejecting God or the Catholic Church. Many humanists were also Christians and attempted to combine their philosophy with church teachings. In his "Oration on the Dignity of Man," Giovanni Pico della Mirandola has God say to Adam:

> We have made thee neither of heaven nor of earth, neither mortal nor immortal, so that with freedom of choice and with honor, as though the maker and molder of thyself, thou mayest fashion thyself in whatever shape thou shalt prefer.[20]

The humanist idea came primarily from two sources, the Catholic Church, which placed the person in a hierarchy beneath God, and the renewed enthusiasm for the study of the ancient Greek and Roman philosophers, who placed a great emphasis on humanity and its role in society. In the Quattrocento these two traditions melded to yield new rules for behavior, politics, and education.

Classical Study

Although the study of ancient Greek and Roman literature, philosophy, and history had never completely died out, such study was aimed primarily at teaching students Latin and supporting the teachings of the Catholic Church. In Italian universities such as the one at Bologna, students were taught Roman law so they could apply it when they became secretaries and lawyers in service to the church or in trade.

In the fourteenth century, Italian scholars began to study the classics for their own sake. The Romans' literary style and secular philosophy was far more developed than that of contemporary writers. Francesco Petrarch (1304–1374), "the father of humanism," especially admired the writings of the Roman orator, politician, and philosopher Cicero. Petrarch wrote:

> From my early youth . . . I gave myself wholly to Cicero. . . . At that age I was incapable of understanding what I read, but I took so much delight in the harmonious disposition of the words that any other book I read or heard read seemed to me to give off a graceless, discordant sound.[21]

Education and scholarship flourished during the Renaissance. In the fourteenth century, Italian scholars revived the study of great classical works, such as the writings of the great Roman Cicero.

In his own writings, Petrarch tried to copy the beautiful rhythms, figures of speech, and the elegant style of the ancient Romans. He came to believe that the way a work was written, its style and form, was just as important as its content. Cultural historian Frederick B. Artz explains:

> Petrarch's place in the history of literary style lies in his emphasis on the idea that formal perfection in literature is of great value in and for itself, that no truth or insight can be dissociated from the artistic perfection of its expression, and that the best guide for the writer is the study of classical literature.[22]

Petrarch shared his love of language and classical scholarship with his disciple Giovanni Boccaccio (1313–1375), another early Renaissance writer. Boccaccio's study of the classics and love of words led him to invent new types of literature in the vernacular, or common language of the people. Among many literary innovations, Boccaccio was responsible for the *Filocopo*, the first Italian prose romance; the *Teseide*, the first romantic Italian epic; and the *Decameron*, the first collection of short stories of literary merit in a vernacular language.

The contributions of Boccaccio and his mentor, Petrarch, were not only literary. Both men studied forgotten classical manuscripts and reintroduced the ideas of ancient writers. They believed that the writings of Cicero and the poets Virgil, Horace, and Ovid, among others, could provide models for human excellence and virtue, and serve as guides for how to live.

Virtue, for these early humanists, was often tied to public service. For example, Cicero, Petrarch's idol, had written:

For all those who have guarded, aided, and increased the welfare of their fatherland there is a place reserved in heaven, where they shall dwell in happiness forever. For . . . there is nothing that is done on earth more acceptable than those meetings for conference of men joined together by the bond of law which are called states. Those who guide and preserve these have come from . . . heaven and to it they return.[23]

Petrarch, therefore, taught that education should serve the public good. He believed that through the study of moral philosophy the student could learn wisdom, and that through the study of rhetoric, the art of speaking and writing

In the burgeoning humanist climate of Renaissance Italy, writer Giovanni Boccaccio invented new types of literature.

well, the student could learn to communicate this knowledge to others. His work stimulated a general interest in ancient ideas. De Lamar Jensen writes:

> By the time of Petrarch's death in 1374, several active groups of men, meeting in the homes of enthusiastic patrons . . . were cultivating the seeds planted by their mentor.[24]

Petrarch's "seeds" were sown all across Italy, but they grew especially well in Florence.

Humanism and the Florentine Platonic Academy

In Florence the growth of humanism was due in part to an influx of teachers from Constantinople, where the ancient Greek heritage had been well preserved. In 1397 Manuel Chrysoloras, a scholar from Constantinople, was invited to teach the Greek language and ideas in Florence. His coming created a great stir among the intellectuals of the time, and students flocked to Chrysoloras to learn about the Greeks. Though Latin and the Roman writers had by then become familiar fare for most scholars, the Greek language and literature had been neglected. Leonardo Bruni, an important humanist of the Quattrocento, explained why he felt the need to study Greek scholarship and language:

> For seven hundred years no one in Italy has known Greek literature, and yet we agree that all language comes from the Greeks. How greatly would familiarity with that language advantage thee in promoting thy knowledge

Human Nature

Renaissance humanists defined a new position for man in relation to God. This excerpt from Giovanni Pico della Mirandola's "Oration on the Dignity of Man," reprinted in The Renaissance Philosophy of Man, *edited by Ernst Cassirer et al., describes the freedom that came with that new definition.*

"The best of artisans [God] ordained that that creature (man) to whom He had been able to give nothing proper to himself should have joint possession of whatever had been peculiar to each of the different kinds of being. He therefore took man as a creature of indeterminate nature and, assigning him a place in the middle of the world, addressed him thus: 'Neither a fixed abode nor a form that is thine alone nor any function peculiar to thyself have we given thee, Adam, to the end that according to thy longing and according to thy judgement thou mayest have and possess what abode, what form, and what functions thou thyself shall desire. . . .Thou, constrained by no limits, in accordance with thine own free will, in whose hand We have placed thee, shall ordain for thyself the limits of thy nature. We have set thee at the world's center that thou mayest from thence more easily observe whatever is in the world. We have made thee neither of heaven nor of earth, neither mortal nor immortal, so that with freedom of choice and with honor, as though the maker and molder of thyself, thou mayest fashion thyself in whatever shape thou shalt prefer.'"

and in the mere increase of thy pleasure? There are teachers of Roman law to be found everywhere . . . but there is but one teacher of Greek, and if he escapes thee there will be no one from whom thou canst learn.[25]

Chrysoloras was followed by other teachers from Constantinople following a 1439 council held in Florence to reconcile the differences between the Eastern Catholic Church, centered in Constantinople, and the Roman Catholic Church, centered in Rome. In 1453, when Constantinople fell to the Turks, still more scholars fled to Florence for refuge.

This influx of scholars may have led to the blossoming of the Florentine Platonic Academy in the middle of the fifteenth century. The academy, under the patronage of Cosimo de' Medici, was a group of intellectuals who met informally to study and discuss ancient Greek philosophy.

Members of the academy were primarily concerned with the teachings of Plato, whose philosophy included a very flattering view of humans. Plato wrote that human reason transcended the ordinary

The Greek philosopher Plato converses with a student in the fourth century B.C. Later, in the fifteenth century, Plato's teachings were revived with the blossoming of the Florentine Platonic Academy.

physical world and connected human beings with an ideal, eternal world. The human mind, if properly trained, could comprehend such abstract ideas as truth, beauty, and justice in their perfect forms.

As a more general program of study, humanism was based in *studia humanitatis* or liberal arts. Unlike earlier secular programs of education, which focused on mathematics and secretarial skills, a liberal arts education focused on history, literary criticism, grammar, poetry, rhetoric, and moral philosophy. The program was meant to give students the skills they needed to contribute to the good of their society.

The humanist program did relatively little to further scientific knowledge. This was not because humanists thought science unimportant, but because they based much of their study on a specific worldview. The humanists believed that nature was spiritual rather than material. For example, many scientists believed that elements of nature such as the earth, sun, ocean, and rain had humanlike spirits. These spirits, rather than being subject to such scientific laws as gravity, responded to human supplication or what could be considered as acts of magic. To understand natural occurrences, Renaissance people quite frequently turned to numerology, the study of magical numbers, and astrology. Notable exceptions included artists who studied mathematics, optics, anatomy, and the natural world of plants and animals to bring more realistic detail to their work.

Even the study of medicine, taught at the universities of Padua and Bologna, combined magic and science in both diagnosis and treatment. The primary concerns of medical students focused on the concepts of "complexion" and "humors." An imbalance in complexions—hot, cold, wet, or dry—was thought to be a result of an imbalance in the four humors—blood, phlegm, red or yellow bile, and black bile. Treatment of illness consisted of restoring balance to the humors which, in turn, would restore balance to the complexion and return the patient to health. For example, bloodletting was one common way of restoring balance to the bodily fluids. Astrology and other forms of magic were also used in diagnosis and treatment. More scientifically, in universities at Padua, Bologna, and Pisa students grew herbs used for treating illnesses and Italian students studied anatomy by dissecting corpses. Through this practice they gained

Francesco Petrarch

Francesco Petrarch, often called the father of humanism, was a respected Renaissance writer and teacher. In the following, quoted in Petrarch, the First Modern Scholar and Man of Letters, *he describes himself in case anyone in future generations should want to know what he was like.*

"Greeting. It is possible that some word of me may have come to you, though even this is doubtful, since an insignificant and obscure name will scarcely penetrate far in either time or space. If, however, you should have heard of me, you may desire to know what manner of man I was. . . .

To begin with myself, then. . . . In my prime I was blessed with a quick and active body, although not exceptionally strong; and while I do not lay claim to remarkable personal beauty, I was comely enough in my best days. I was possessed of a clear complexion, between light and dark, lively eyes, and for long years a keen vision, which however deserted me, contrary to my hopes, after I reached my sixtieth birthday, and forced me, to my great annoyance, to resort to glasses. . . . I possessed a well-balanced rather than a keen intellect. . . . Among the many subjects which interested me, I dwelt especially upon antiquity, for our own age has always repelled me, so that, had it not been for the love of those dear to me, I should have preferred to have been born in any other period than our own."

Francesco Petrarch, Italian poet and early humanist, is often called the father of humanism.

greater knowledge of the human body and its functions.

Within the context of humanist teaching, great strides were made in the area of astronomy. Nicolaus Copernicus, though born in Poland, completed his studies at schools in Ferrara, Bologna, and Padua. In his 1530 work *De revolutionibus orbium coelestium* (*On the Revolutions of the Celestial Spheres*) Copernicus concluded that both sun and stars were motionless in the heavens, and that the earth and planets revolved around the sun. His work, though it did not have an immediate impact on other scientists, raised questions which scientists attempted to answer in the following century.

Dissatisfied with the prevailing earth-centered cosmology, Nicolaus Copernicus formulated his theory that the earth orbited a stationary sun. His ideas paved the way for future scientists.

Printing and the Spread of Ideas

Advances in technology had a greater impact in the Renaissance than did science. The ideas of humanism spread quickly due to improvements in printing capability brought on by Johannes Gutenberg of Mainz, Germany. Gutenberg is generally credited with the invention of movable type printing between 1445 and 1450. Though printing technology had been in use in Europe since the twelfth century, before Gutenberg the process was arduous and very slow. Early printers had to hand carve each letter of each page backwards on a block of wood used to make impressions on paper. Every new book or pamphlet required all new blocks. Even a single book might require repeated carvings if the wooden blocks wore out after many impressions.

With Gutenberg's new movable type the process was much easier. Printers cast individual letters out of metal, which could be arranged and rearranged as needed in a case or plate, and then reused. The improvements revolutionized the process of printing.

The first printing press with movable type in Italy was established in a monastery near Rome in 1464, and by 1480 every city-state had its own printing presses. By 1500 Venice, which excelled in the new technology, boasted almost one hundred printers (a total greater than that of all the other city-states combined) and had printed nearly two million documents in twenty years.

One of the most important Venetian presses was the Aldine. Owned by the humanist scholar Aldo Mannucci, the Aldine

Johannes Gutenberg revolutionized the printing process with the invention of movable type. For the first time, books were available to wide audiences, stimulating a proliferation of ideas.

Press specialized in printing Greek classics, which were reproduced as small, relatively inexpensive books that scholars could both afford and carry. Through Mannucci, more and more students were exposed to Aristotle, Sophocles, and many other giants of the classical age.

The Humanist Elite

In Florence in the middle of the Quattrocento, young people who studied the humanities most often came from wealthy families. Writes Gene Brucker: "By the middle of the fifteenth century, many houses—Strozzi, Corbinelli, Rossi, Medici, Davanzati, Allesandri—could . . . boast of a humanist scholar."[26] Such young people hired private tutors to come to their homes or met in monasteries or private houses to read and discuss classical texts. Rich and influential, many went on to hold high political office and perform important government services. Often they were sought to fill ambassadorial positions.

Though diplomacy, the art of negotiation, had its roots in earlier times, it came to fruition in the Quattrocento. Because Italy was not a unified country and city-states developed widely varied forms of government, clashes over political beliefs and competition for resources often had the potential to end in war. War, however, was costly and depleted the resources of a city-state. Diplomacy offered a less expensive alternative; gradually leaders of city-states discovered they could communicate with each other and sometimes resolve their differences peacefully through the negotiations of representatives called diplomats.

Duty

During the early Renaissance people had more freedom to explore their relationship with God and with each other. With this freedom came certain responsibilities, as humanist Marsilio Ficino explained in a letter, reprinted in The Letters of Marsilio Ficino, *to his friend Cherubino Quarguagli in 1476.*

"Duty is the action proper to each man, which keeps to what is fitting and honourable as circumstance, person, place and time require.

The virtue and duty of the priest are wisdom that glows with piety, and a piety that shines with wisdom. The duty of the prince is to watch over all; mercy in justice, humility in greatness and greatness in humility. The duty of the magistrate is to remember that he is not the master but the servant of the law, and the public guardian of the state; furthermore, that while he is judging men he is being judged by God. The duty of the private individual is to obey the magistrates' commands so willingly that he seems not to be compelled by the necessity of the law but to be led by his own will. The duty of the citizen, whether he be a magistrate or private individual, is to care as greatly for the public interest as he greatly cherishes his own. The duty of the knight is bravery in war and noble action in peace; of the merchant, with true faith and diligence to nourish both the state and himself with good things from abroad."

Milan led the way in establishing permanent residences for their diplomats in other city-states. By the beginning of the fifteenth century it maintained embassies in Florence, Venice, and Naples. As the century progressed Milan expanded outside Italy to include France and other European countries in its diplomatic network. By the second half of the Quattrocento having permanent embassies in other cities and countries was common for most Italian city-states.

Diplomatic positions were very important. Ambassadors negotiated with the heads of other city-states, maneuvered against the enemies of their own governments, and collected information sent home to give their own leaders any possible advantage. They also represented their city-states in public events.

To be an ambassador required good communication skills above all else. As part of their training in rhetoric, humanist students learned the art of communication and persuasion in both speech and writing, most valuable skills in embassies. Not only did they have the skills they needed to negotiate with the heads of rival city-states, they were capable of making accurate accounts of events and sending that information back home.

These skills were also important in other branches of government and positions of influence. Humanists acted as secretaries and cultural and political advisers, taking prominent roles in government. Leonardo Bruni worked as an adviser and resident scholar in the courts of four popes. Lorenzo Valla, a student of Bruni, was secretary to King Alfonso of Naples. Between 1375 and 1459 four humanists—Colluccio Salutati, Leonardo Bruni, Carlo Marsuppini, and Poggio Bracciolini—served as chancellor in Florence.

In these positions of influence humanists promoted their philosophy, and under their guidance Italy flourished. Historian Francesco Guicciardini (1483–1540), in *The History of Italy*, described Italy at the end of the Quattrocento:

It is obvious that ever since the Roman Empire . . . Italy had never enjoyed such prosperity, or known so favorable a situation as that in which it found itself so securely at rest in the year of our Christian salvation, 1490, and the years immediately before and after.

The greatest peace and tranquility reigned everywhere; the land under cultivation no less in the most mountainous and arid regions than in the most fertile plains and areas; dominated by no power other than her own, not only did Italy abound in inhabitants, merchandise and riches, but she was also highly renowned for the magnificence of many princes, for the splendor of so many noble and beautiful cities, as the seat and majesty of religion, and flourishing with men most skilled in the administration of public affairs and most nobly talented in all the disciplines and distinguished and industrious in all the arts. Nor was Italy lacking in so many gifts that she deservedly held a celebrated name and reputation among all nations.[27]

Italy was perhaps not as perfect as Guicciardini remembered it, but the Quattrocento was one of the truly "golden ages" in European history. The humanists had created a dynamic cultural milieu in which education, interwoven with politics, allowed for innovations that would affect the entire world in the following centuries.

Chapter

4 Art and Architecture of the Early Renaissance

Of all the achievements of the Quattrocento, none equaled the great strides made in the art and architecture of Florence. Under the patronage of the communal government and such rich and powerful families as the Medici, Renaissance artists and their arts flourished. The architect Filippo Brunelleschi, designer of the giant dome of Florence's Cathedral of Santa Maria del Fiore (Holy Mary of the Flower) is credited with introducing artists to the rules of linear perspective. The painter Masaccio, using Brunelleschi's technique, created an illusion of reality in his wall paintings that outstripped even the great pre-Renaissance artist Giotto's work. The sculptor Donatello produced the first freestanding, life-size nude in Europe since antiquity, and Sandro Botticelli brought ancient myths to life on canvas for his most important patron, Lorenzo de' Medici.

Great Patrons of Art

Rich Florentine families such as the Medici were some of the most active patrons of the day. For their own aggrandizement, they often commissioned private chapels, elaborate tombs, and works of religious art. Often displayed in prominent

places, these works were manifestations of the donor's power, wealth, and importance. Cosimo de' Medici, for example, financed the reconstruction of many churches and monasteries during his lifetime, including San Lorenzo, San Marco, and the Badia of Fiesole.

Other patrons commissioned smaller projects no less effective in reflecting their prominence in their city. It was not unusual for portraits of donors to appear in religious paintings alongside representations of Christ, Mary, and the saints. In a wall painting by Masaccio in Florence's Church of Santa Maria Novella, the two figures kneeling at the outer edges of the scene are those of the couple who paid for the painting, a merchant and his wife.

The city-state government also used the arts to demonstrate the power and importance of Florence. It provided money for constructing and decorating great cathedrals such as Santa Maria del Fiore, and joined other groups, such as trade guilds or societies devoted to religious causes, in supporting large community projects.

For the trade guilds patronage involved competition as well as pride in craftsmanship and a love of art. Often they would try to outdo one another in the beauty and costliness of the works they commissioned or supervised. In 1425, at a meeting of the

Advice to Painters

Early Renaissance artists depended on the support of patrons for their livelihood. In the following excerpt from his book On Painting, *Leon Battista Alberti, an early Renaissance scholar, artist, and architect, advises painters on how to win patron support.*

"Since there are other useful things which will make a painter such that he can attain to perfect fame, we should not omit them in this commentary. We will treat of them most briefly. . . . I would be delighted if the painter . . . should be a good man and learned in liberal arts. Everyone knows how much more the goodness of a man is worth than all his industry or art in acquiring the benevolence of the citizens. No one doubts that the good will of many is a great help to the artist in acquiring both fame and wealth. It often happens that the rich, moved more by amiability than by love of the arts, reward first one who is modest and good, leaving behind another painter perhaps better in art but not so good in his habits. Therefore the painter ought to acquire many good habits—principally humanity and affability. He will thus have a firm aid against poverty in good will, the greatest aid in learning his art well."

council of the Lana guild of cloth workers, members learned that a church tabernacle they had commissioned was not as nice as those commissioned by other guilds. Horrified, they decided to rebuild the work so that it would "exceed, or at least equal, in beauty and decoration the more beautiful ones [built by other guilds]." [28]

Humanism and the Arts

Humanism influenced the types of work commissioned by wealthy art patrons. Over the course of the Renaissance patrons came to prefer and commission works that demonstrated harmony, balance, proportion, and symmetry—that is, the formal classical ideals. In order to please their patrons and themselves, early Renaissance artists looked to the past for their models of perfection. In the fifteenth century, architect and sculptor Filippo Brunelleschi, for example, traveled to Rome to study the ancient buildings and ruins of the Roman civilization. Giorgio Vasari (1511–1574), a Renaissance art historian, wrote that when Brunelleschi first saw the ruins of Rome, "he stood there so engrossed in thought that he seemed to be beside himself with amazement." [29]

Brunelleschi incorporated what he learned from studying the ruins in his own work. His most important contribution to architecture was the giant dome on top of

Even today, the domed profile of the Santa Maria del Fiore dominates the skyline of Florence (top). The construction of the dome was a major achievement, marking the beginning of Renaissance architecture in Florence. (Left) The interior of the cathedral.

Santa Maria del Fiore. Combining medieval techniques of church building, his knowledge of classical style, and his own genius, he introduced a new kind of architecture.

The Dome of Santa Maria del Fiore

Work on Santa Maria del Fiore was begun in 1296, during the Middle Ages. The Florentine communal government provided most of the money for the cathedral, and the Lana guild of cloth manufacturers supervised its construction. Eight generations of Florentine artists worked on the building, the most well known of whom was Giotto, who designed a portion of the cathedral's bell tower in 1334.

Almost from the beginning the Florentines envisioned a huge dome atop the cathedral that would be the envy of all of Italy and bring the city the respect and admiration it sought. The problem was that no one had the expertise to build it. The 140-foot opening was so wide architects could not use the traditional wooden framework to span it during construction. It was also believed that the weight of such a large dome would be unsupportable, surely causing it to cave in.

In 1365 an artist painted a picture of what the completed dome would look like, but still no one knew how it could be done. Preparations for its construction continued, however, and builders began work on its base. The base was completed in 1413, but still there was no workable design for the dome. The planners were in a quandary. They called in both Italian and non-Italian architects, who bitterly disputed how the dome could be built. Many felt the project was impossible.

After much debate, in 1417 the Florentines decided it was time to at least try. They commissioned Brunelleschi to attempt the task and, to the amazement of many, he solved the problem. He designed two interior shells, the inner one of masonry and the outer one of tiles, which would lessen the heavy weight of the dome on the foundation of the building. The shells had interconnecting rib supports between them, which would eventually be anchored by a lantern at the top. In addition, the dome was constructed in layers, the lower layers providing support for those above.

Brunelleschi's design worked. The dome was dedicated in 1436, amidst great celebration in Florence. Art historian William Fleming writes:

> March 25, 1436, was a special occasion that would linger long in the memory of these prosperous and pleasure-loving people. The dedication of Florence's newly completed cathedral brought together an unprecedented number of Church dignitaries, statesmen, and diplomats, and in their wake were famous artists, poets, scholars and musicians. The white-robed Pope Eugene IV, crowned with the triple tiara, attended by 7 cardinals in bright red and no fewer than 37 bishops and archbishops in purple vestments, made a triumphal progress through the banner-lined streets, accompanied by city officials and heads of the guilds with their honor guards.[30]

The dome marked the beginning of Renaissance architecture in Florence, a style that would influence public and church building into the twentieth century. Vasari echoed the thoughts of many when he wrote that the dome was "the greatest, tallest, and most beautiful structure" the world had ever seen.[31]

A New Perspective

The dome was not Brunelleschi's only contribution to Renaissance art. He is generally given credit for discovering a technique known as linear perspective. In linear perspective, a flat, two-dimensional work of art is like a framed window opening onto a separate, three-dimensional world with its own spatial and distance relationships. Figures are arranged along parallel lines that converge and seem to radiate from a single place on the horizon called the vanishing point. For example, in an avenue of trees, the trees that are supposed to be closest to the viewer are drawn largest, where the lines are farthest apart, and the ones that are supposed to be more distant are drawn smaller and smaller, as they get closer to the vanishing point. This gives the illusion that the avenue is fading away into the distance.

This technique influenced many early Renaissance artists, especially painters.

Masaccio, one of the greatest painters of the Quattrocento, incorporated linear perspective in his work and combined it with other techniques to create a new level of realism in art. He improved on Giotto's technique in his use of light and shade. His paintings look as if they were lit from outside the work by a single light source. Light seems to strike the painted figures at an angle, brightening certain parts of figures, and casting deep shadows behind them. Where Giotto had created volume and depth with light and shadow, Masaccio created the illusion of real mass in real space.

Brunelleschi's Persistence

When the committee in charge of building Santa Maria del Fiore decided the time had come to attempt the great dome, they summoned architects from both Italy and foreign parts. Brunelleschi's ideas were at first dismissed, as his Renaissance biographer Antonio di Tuccio Manetti describes in the following passage from The Life of Brunelleschi.

"Not having proved himself in any large undertaking comparable to this building, and this building having to be such as it later appeared and as was then anticipated—and not having sufficient influence at that time to satisfy everyone, he was ridiculed by the [committee] and other ordinary citizens and no less by our own masters than by the foreign masters. . . . The [committee] unanimously drew the conclusion that a large building of such a character could not be completed. . . . When Filippo protested against this erroneous conclusion . . . and . . . told them it could be done, they united in one in asking: How will it be supported? He repeated constantly that it could be vaulted. . . . After many days of standing firm—he in his opinion and they in theirs—he was twice angrily carried out by the servants of the [committee] . . . as if he were reasoning foolishly and his words were laughable. As a consequence he was later often wont to say that during the period . . . he was ashamed to go about Florence. He had the feeling that behind his back they were saying: Look at that mad man who utters such nonsense."

The young painter also rediscovered aerial perspective, an ancient Roman technique for creating distance. In this kind of perspective objects that are supposed to appear more distant seem less distinct than those that are supposed to appear close to the viewer—as if clouded by air and moisture. By combining this kind of perspective with linear perspective and the illusion of a single light source, Masaccio's paintings were more lifelike than any before his time.

The young artist's ability to adapt, synthesize, and invent techniques set a new standard in painting. His work paved the way for High Renaissance artists such as Leonardo da Vinci, Michelangelo, and Raphael, who would bring still more life to two-dimensional surfaces.

Florentine sculptor Donatello's mastery of realism is apparent in works such as St. Mark.

Sculpture

Much early Renaissance art was religious. Artists and architects such as Brunelleschi and Masaccio were commissioned to build and decorate Florentine churches and chapels, such as Santa Maria del Fiore, Santo Spirito, the Pazzi Chapel, Santa Maria Novella, and Santa Maria del Carmine. The content of church and chapel decorations was religious, depicting traditional themes such as the Crucifixion, Adam and Eve being expelled from the Garden of Eden, and Mary with the Christ child.

The style in which artists sculpted and painted these figures, however, was more and more often secular. Jesus, Mary, and other religious figures no longer appeared aloof, untouchable, and otherworldly. They looked more human and real than in the past. The postures and expressions of painted and sculpted faces seemed to reflect real human emotions such as sorrow, tenderness, or suffering. Even more than Giotto, early Renaissance artists attempted to depict the human condition, even when the subject matter was Christ, Mary, and the saints.

The third great artist of the early Renaissance, the sculptor Donatello, was particularly adept at creating lifelike statues. His early works focused intensely on the human nature of his subjects, their physicality, their vibrant vitality, and their psychology. Even his biblical figures resembled people one could meet in the streets of Florence. They stand in natural postures and their human personalities are reflected in their faces. This is apparent in works such as *St. Mark* in the San Michele, a church in Florence.

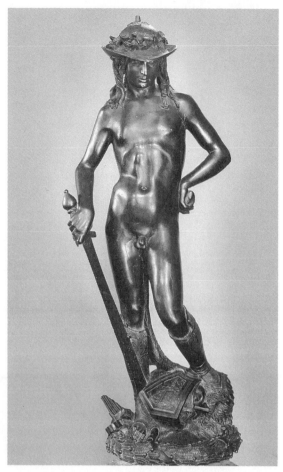

Donatello further advanced the new realism when he created the first free-standing nude in Western art since antiquity, his bronze David.

The glance of this youthful, still adolescent hero is not directed primarily toward the severed head of Goliath, which lies between his feet, but toward his own graceful, sinuous body, as though . . . becoming conscious for the first time of its beauty, its vitality, and its strength. This self-awareness, this discovery of self, is the dominant theme in Renaissance art.[32]

By resurrecting the nude and placing a greater emphasis on the grace of the human figure, Donatello set a new standard in sculpture. His work would continue to be perfected in the High Renaissance by artists such as Michelangelo, whose own statue of David would become one of the most famous works of art in history.

Renaissance Patrons

Novel styles of art were eagerly sought after by the rich and influential people of the day to fill their sumptuous palaces. During the early Renaissance in Florence, there was a great flurry of palace building and improvement. The Medici, the Pitti, and the Strozzi, among others, built new homes. Families such as the Lapi and Spinelli remodeled their old ones in the classical style. The sounds of construction added to the bustle of Florence, sometimes to the great inconvenience of the shopkeepers. The apothecary Luca Landucci, whose shop was across the street from the new Strozzi palace, describes the annoyance of the building process. On August 20, 1489, he wrote in his diary:

All the streets around were filled with heaps of stone and rubbish . . . making

Donatello also resurrected the ancient classical nude, which had, except for scenes depicting the Garden of Eden or hell, been banned by the Catholic Church. His bronze *David*, the giant slayer from the Old Testament, was the first free-standing nude statue in western Europe since antiquity. Unlike the ancient statues, however, Donatello's *David*, in the humanist tradition, seems to be aware of himself as a person. Art historian Helen Gardner writes:

it difficult for anyone to pass along. We shopkeepers were continually annoyed by the dust and the crowds of people who collected to look on.[33]

These new palaces incorporated the classical principles of order, symmetry, and proportion and displayed such classical features as columns, arches, and capitals, the decorative upper parts of columns, which had been popular in ancient Greece and Rome. The new palaces were also more spacious than the old ones, and they provided room and a backdrop for rich Florentines to display their wealth. The Medici, in particular, used their grand homes to impress others with Medici power. They filled their palaces with antiques, works of art, and costly furnishings.

Many of these works were nonreligious. Secular themes and styles were becoming more popular in the Renaissance, though they were not yet as numerous as religious works. Patrons commissioned landscapes, portraits, mythological themes, and depictions of the lives of the wealthy.

Sandro Botticelli, who lived from about 1444 to 1510, was one artist who quite often painted nonreligious works. Botticelli, a favorite of patron Lorenzo de' Medici, studied Plato's philosophy at the Florentine Platonic Academy, where his friends and teachers were some of the most important humanists of the day.

Often commissioned by Lorenzo de Medici, the works of Sandro Botticelli (left) are considered some of the greatest ever painted. Botticelli's attention to detail and emphasis on the classical past are clearly revealed in the detail from Primavera *(right).*

With its graceful and rhythmic lines, Botticelli's Birth of Venus *is among the most famous paintings of the Renaissance.*

From them he learned a deep respect for the past and became particularly interested in classical mythology. The stories of the ancient gods and goddesses provided the themes for many of Botticelli's works. His *Birth of Venus*, which shows the goddess rising out of the sea on a shell, is one of the most well known paintings of the early Renaissance. That this Venus was nude marks a milestone in the history of painting. Writes Helen Gardner:

> The presentation of the figure of Venus nude was, in itself, an innovation. . . . Its appearance on such a scale

[the painting is 5'8" x 9'1"] and its use of an ancient Venus statue . . . as a model could have drawn the charge of paganism and infidelity. But under the protection of the powerful Medici, a new world of imagination could open freely with the new Platonism.[34]

Painters, sculptors, and architects were not the only artists to borrow from the classical tradition and use ancient themes and forms as their models. During the fourteenth century dramatists wrote plays in the style of such classical playwrights as Seneca, Terence, and Plautus. In 1315 Albertino Mussato combined Christian subject matter with a modified classical form to write the tragedy *Eccerinus*. Antonio Laschi's *Achilles* (ca. 1390) is considered to be the first Renaissance tragedy because it combined both classical form and subject matter in a single play.

Comedies reappeared in Italy in the late fourteenth and early fifteenth centuries. Pier Paolo Vergio's *Paulus*, a satire on student life written in 1390, was among the first. Many humanists followed in his footsteps but none of their works had much literary merit and most are generally considered uninteresting by modern scholars.

Most of these early plays were written in Latin and not many were performed. Even the classical plays which had been discovered in the rush to uncover ancient manuscripts were not produced until 1486, when the Roman Academy began experimenting with staging. Ferrara and other courts throughout Italy soon followed the academy's lead, and staged their own plays.

Because many of the most renowned artists and architects of the day were also employed to create sets for these plays, perspective was introduced into set design. Though many scholars believe the technique was used as early as the 1480s,

Patron Rivalry

Commissioning beautiful works of art for the city of Florence was a matter of pride for many patrons. In the following excerpt, taken from Gene Brucker's The Society of Renaissance Florence, *members of the Lana guild, in 1425, embarrassed because other guilds had built more beautiful tabernacles for a church, decide to try again.*

"The consuls [of the Lana guild] have considered that all of the guilds have finished their tabernacles, and that those constructed by the Calimala and Cambio guilds, and by other guilds, surpass in beauty and ornamentation that of the Lana guild. So it may be truly said that this does not redound to the honor of the Lana guild, particularly when one considers the magnificence of that guild which has always sought to be the master and the superior of the other guilds.

For the splendor and honor of the guild, the lord consuls desire . . . to construct, fabricate, and remake a tabernacle and a statue of the blessed Stephen, protomartyr, protector and defender of the renowned Lana guild, in his honor and in reverence to God. They are to do this by whatever ways and means they choose, which will most honorably contribute to the splendor of the guild, so that this tabernacle will exceed, or at least equal, in beauty and decoration the more beautiful ones."

there is no official record of it appearing until 1508 in a production of Lodovico Ariosto's *The Casket*, performed in Ferrara.

Renaissance Music

Italian musicians did not achieve the same renown as their fellow literary and visual artists. Between 1420 and 1490 there were very few Italian composers of any note working in Italy. Some scholars believe this was because it became fashionable for wealthy Italians to import musicians from northern Europe. For example, the northern European composer Dufay, who wrote the dedication motet for Brunelleschi's

Lodovico Ariosto (pictured) wrote The Casket, *which was the first production that featured perspective in set design.*

dome, was also commissioned to create works for the Malatesta family in Pesaro and Rimini, and for the popes in Rome. In Florence Lorenzo de' Medici employed Heinrich Isaac, Alexander Agricola, and Johannes Ghiselin, all Flemish singer-composers. The Sforza family in Milan commissioned works by such northern musicians as Josquin des Prez, Johannes Martini, Gaspar van Weerbeke and Loyset Compere.

As in the other arts, humanism had an impact on music. However, unlike in literature, architecture, and sculpture there were no existing models for composers to follow in trying to re-create classical forms. Often composers took literature and architecture as their models. For example, when creating his motet for Brunelleschi's dome, Dufay tried to echo the classical, orderly style of the cupola—to translate the visual into the musical. In one passage he has two tenor voices enter at specific intervals that would seem to have mathematical relationships similar to those used in the double-vaulted dome.

Believing that in ancient times the poet and the composer had been one, poets attempted to make their writings more musical, concentrating on the sound of their words. Composers, in turn, attempted to imitate, in music, the sound of the words as they would have been spoken. This required special attention to the punctuation and syntax of the text, which would then be echoed in the melody and rhythm of the composition.

A renaissance in music occurred in Italy in the early sixteenth century with the development of the madrigal. Though in the fourteenth century there had been a form of music called madrigal, it had almost nothing in common with that which developed in Italy in the early sixteenth century. The fourteenth-century madrigal was strophic; that is, it had a verse and refrain, which allowed the music to repeat itself. In the sixteenth century the Italians dropped the refrain and almost all other features of the old madrigal. Their madrigals were nonstrophic, and the music did not contain repeats. The melody unfolded from beginning to end in a more intricate form. From 1520 to 1550 Renaissance madrigals required four voices, with one singer assigned to one musical line. As the century progressed the number of voices expanded, and a madrigal might employ six, eight, or even ten voices. Initially texts for Italian madrigals were most often taken from the writings of Petrarch, whose beautiful language inspired composers to set the master's lyrical words to song. Later madrigal writers used texts written by lesser poets in the style of Petrarch.

Madrigals became very popular throughout Italy. They were performed at court gatherings and at intellectual academies. Between 1530 and 1600 approximately two thousand collections of madrigals were printed and distributed in Italy.

Innovations in printing made copies of musical compositions more available to a wider variety of people. In 1501 the Venetian Ottaviano de' Petrucci printed collections of music using movable type. By 1523 his press had published fifty-nine volumes of both vocal and instrumental music. This meant that accurate copies of original compositions could reach performers throughout Italy and the north.

The Renaissance in literature, the visual arts, dramatic performance and music, then, developed at different rates, according to various influences, patterns of patronage, and the specific requirements of the art. This staggered progression was similar to the development of the city-states themselves. Being autonomous regions affected by diverse geographical and political factors, not all areas of Italy experienced the Renaissance at the same time. The cultural revolution in Rome, for example, was many decades behind the Renaissance in Florence.

5 Rome and French Invasions of Italy

While Florence thrived in the early Renaissance, Rome was crumbling in a sad state of neglect and disrepair. In 1420 only twenty-five thousand people lived in a city built to hold nearly a million. Much of the dwindled population settled in a bend near the Tiber River, where, though they were subject to floods, lowland heat, and disease, they could get drinking water. The city's nobility, old and once powerful families, lived in the ruins of ancient public buildings, which they had fortified as strongholds.

The walled city, which was nearly fourteen miles in circumference, was more like open country than a great seat of power. Robbers, outlaws, and wild animals took shelter in large patches of wilderness. A Spanish traveler of the time wrote: "There are parts within the walls which look like thick woods, and wild beasts, hares, foxes, deer and even so it is said porcupines breed in the caves."[35]

A City in Trouble

In parts of the city that were more tame, Romans grazed their cows and grew grapes amid the crumbling ruins of what had once been one of the greatest cities in the world. In the 1420s the humanist writer Poggio Bracciolini described the Rome of his day:

> The Forum of the Roman people is now enclosed for the cultivation of pot-herbs, or thrown for the reception of swine and buffalo. The public and private edifices that were founded for eternity lie prostrate, naked and broken, like the limb of a mighty giant, and the ruin is more obvious because of the stupendous relics that have survived the injuries of time and fortune.[36]

One reason for Rome's decay was that, traditionally, it did not have a strong industrial or commercial base. The bulk of its food and manufactured goods had been imported. Rome's wine came from Corsica, Naples, and Crete. Romans purchased their cloth from Florence, their soap from Genoa, and their paper from Fabriano. Their carpets came from Turkey and their swords from Milan. The merchant and middle classes, who had done so much to build cities like Florence and bring stability to the northern states, had not developed in Rome.

The city's economic and political power had always come from the strength and wealth of the Catholic Church. When a pope was in residence, papal revenues poured in and filled its coffers. Pilgrims came from all over Europe to worship in the Eternal City, and to spend their money on room and board and souvenirs of their journey. The literate and urbane clergy who served the church also brought prosperity and energy to the community when a pope was in Rome.

The Avignon Papacy (1311–1377) and the Great Schism (1378–1417) had greatly damaged the city. The absence of a pope in Rome and then the confusion of multiple popes had robbed the city of its income and eroded its position as a world power. Church cardinals of the time estimated that the Great Schism had cost the papacy one-third of its revenues. When Martin V, the first Renaissance pope, returned to Rome in 1420, he was faced with the task of restoring the city's power and glory on a relatively small budget.

Taming Rome

Lack of money, however, was not the only problem awaiting Martin when he brought the united papacy back to Rome. During the Great Schism, rival popes had fought over who would reside there. In the confusion, control of Rome passed from the hands of mercenary soldiers to the duke of Milan to the king of Naples.

Rome also had its own communal government, which, throughout the Schism, vied with the pope for control of the city. Often supported by rich and powerful families, the commune frequently challenged the weakened popes' authority. For example, in 1398, the Colonna, Caetani, and Savelli families attempted to launch an insurrection against Boniface IX. In 1404

The Decay of Rome

In the early fifteenth century, Rome had fallen into neglect and disrepair. Poggio Bracciolini, a humanist writer, described its decay in The Inconstancy of Fortune, *quoted in* The Portable Renaissance Reader.

"It is indeed most grievous and scarcely to be related without great amazement that this Capitoline hill, once the head and center of the Roman Empire . . . now lies so desolated and ruined . . . that vines have replaced the benches of the senators, and the Capitol has become a receptacle of dung and filth. Look at the Palatine . . . [once] embellished with the assembled riches of the empire . . . admired by all who beheld it; all this is now so ruined that not a shadow remains that can be identified as anything but wild wasteland. Look at the other hills of the city. You see them all lying forsaken, their buildings ruined and overgrown with vines. The forum, which . . . was the most famous place in the city . . . has become . . . a neglected desert, here the home of pigs and wild deer, and there a vegetable garden."

the king of Naples had to be called in to mediate a dispute between Pope Innocent VII and the commune over control of the city. The commune won and its authority was restored to the detriment of the pope.

Martin entered the tangled politics of Rome with at least two advantages, however. The Schism had ended and he was the sole pope of Christendom. And he was a Roman from the powerful Colonna family. With the help of his kin, he managed, for a time, to reestablish papal authority in the city and brighten Rome's prospects. Historian J. H. Plumb writes:

> With the papal court back in Rome, back came the pilgrims and supplicants, back came the merchants, and back came the lifeblood—the papal tax harvest that was reaped from Europe's peasantry. And so the Roman soil was fertilized again, for without wealth no Renaissance was possible.[37]

Martin's efforts, however, did not permanently secure Rome for the popes. His successor, Eugenius IV, was a Venetian and did not have the strength of a powerful Roman family to back him up. In 1434, threatened by warring mercenaries from central Italy, he was forced to flee Rome in a rowboat and he spent most of the following decade in Florence and Bologna.

Eugenius's forced flight taught the popes who followed him an important lesson. They realized that in order to maintain possession of Rome they had to control the territories around it.

The Papal States

The Papal States were a diverse group of territories stretching in a band across cen-

Because Eugenius IV (seated center) lacked control of the territories around Rome, he was forced to flee the city. His forced exile prompted future popes to strengthen their yoke of control across Italy.

tral Italy from the kingdom of Naples in the south to Siena, Florence, Modena, and Ferrara in the north. To the south of Rome lay the Papal States of Campagna and Marittima. The Patrimony of St. Peter was to Rome's north, and Sabina, Spoleto, the March of Ancona, and Romagna spread east and north. Important cities in the Papal States included Bologna, Ferrara, Ancona, Perugia, and Spoleto. Now the political stabilization of the Papal States became a top priority for the Renaissance popes.

The territories and cities of the Papal States had diverse forms of government. Bologna, Perugia, and Ancona, for the most part, maintained communal rule. In other areas powerful families, whose vast estates provided them with economic and military might, were in control. For example, the Montefeltro dukes of Urbino controlled mountain passes between Rome and the cities of the northeast, and the powerful Sforza had control of Pesaro on the Adriatic Sea.

If the popes could bring these areas under control, not only would they gain security against attack, they would increase their revenues as well. As overlords of the Papal States, they could tax the territories and bring badly needed income to Rome. In addition, the Papal States could provide basic necessities such as firewood and foodstuffs to a city that traditionally could not support itself.

Nepotism

The popes had a spiritual motivation in controlling the Papal States. They believed that the land that stretched across central Italy had once belonged to Saint Peter, the first pope. Historian Charles L. Stinger explains:

> These territories, the popes believed, constituted the "patrimony" of Peter. That is, they belonged to the saint himself, and therefore to the Roman church. The popes thus had a sacred duty to prevent their falling into alien hands.[38]

With so much at stake—security, income, and the heritage of Saint Peter—

Renaissance popes, for the most part, were not selected for their spiritual qualities, but for their political abilities and administrative talent. One strategy that proved especially helpful in papal politics was nepotism, the practice of elevating family members to positions of power. De Lamar Jensen explains: "Papal dynasticism depended on having enough right people in the right places at the right times."[39]

Beginning with Sixtus IV (1471–1484) nepotism, already prevalent in Rome, became rampant. Once elected, he raised five of his nephews to the status of cardinal and granted them immense power in the Papal States. Giuliano della Rovere (who would become Pope Julius II in 1503) gained jurisdiction over Bologna,

The reign of Pope Sixtus IV, elected to the papacy in 1471, was characterized by rampant nepotism.

Lausanne, and Constance. Piero Riario was given the direction of papal politics. Girolamo Riario, son-in-law of the duke of Milan, was made cardinal and Giovanni della Rovere became the prefect of Rome.

Innocent VIII (1484–1492) and Alexander VI (1492–1503) also practiced nepotism. In 1489 Innocent elevated his nephew Giovanni de' Medici (Pope Leo X), the fourteen-year-old son of Lorenzo, to the office of cardinal. Alexander used the papacy to promote the political career of his son Cesare Borgia and to make advantageous marriages for his daughter Lucrezia.

Partially through the practice of nepotism, the popes consolidated power in the Papal States and, therefore, in Rome. By the end of the fifteenth century, the popes had control of urban planning, public works, and city finances. Important administrative offices and key positions of power were held by papal authorities—often papal relatives.

Nepotism, however, was not the only tool they used to gain the upper hand. Along with political astuteness and military acumen, a new form of humanism aided the popes in their quest for power.

Roman Humanism

The humanism that developed in Rome differed distinctly from the type popular in other parts of Italy. Roman humanists looked to ancient Rome for their inspiration. Their goal was to establish Rome as the dominant city of Europe with an emperor-like pope governing Italy and all of Christendom.

Many Renaissance popes encouraged the growth of this kind of thinking.

Nicholas V (1447–1455) hired leading humanists to translate Greek texts into Latin and assembled a first-rate library housed at the Vatican. Using the Roman Empire as his ideal, he began rebuilding Rome's ancient churches, and made plans for a new Vatican city that would be the most fabulous in all of Christendom. Nicholas, during his pontificate, worked on both the Vatican and the city of Rome. He commissioned the building of several private and public palaces, paved many of the streets of Rome, and promoted the restoration of churches, palaces, and the Milvian bridge.

This quest for glory, Pope Nicholas claimed, was not secular, but spiritual. On

Nicholas V encouraged the growth of Roman humanism, seeking to establish Rome as the dominant city in all of Christendom.

Advice to a Young Cardinal

At the turn of the fifteenth century Rome had become known as a den of iniquity. In a letter of advice to his son Giovanni (who would become Pope Leo X), a newly made cardinal, Lorenzo de' Medici warned the young man of the dangers he would face in the Holy City. In a letter written shortly before his death, reprinted in Will Durant's The Renaissance, *Lorenzo wrote:*

"I well know that as you are now to reside at Rome, that sink of all iniquity, the difficulty of conducting yourself by these admonitions will be increased. The influence of example is itself prevalent; but you will probably meet with those who will particularly endeavor to corrupt and incite you to vice; because, as you may yourself perceive, your early attainment to so great a dignity is not observed without envy, and those who could not prevent your receiving that honor will secretly endeavor to diminish it, by inducing you to forfeit the good estimation of the public; and thereby precipitating you into that gulf into which they have themselves fallen; in which attempt the consideration of your youth will give them a confidence of success. To these difficulties you ought to oppose yourself with the greater firmness as there is at present less virtue amongst your brethren of the college [of cardinals]. . . . Avoid . . . the imputation of hypocrisy; guard against all ostentation, either in your conduct or in your discourse; affect not austerity, nor even appear too serious. This advice you will, I hope, in time understand better than I can express it."

his deathbed he is alleged to have explained:

To create solid and stable convictions in the minds of the uncultured masses, there must be something which appeals to the eye; a popular faith sustained only on doctrines, will never be anything but feeble and vacillating. But if the authority of the Holy See were visibly displayed in majestic buildings, imperishable memorials and witnesses seemingly planted by the hand of God himself, belief would grow and strengthen from one generation to another, and all the world would accept and revere it.[40]

Moreover, Nicholas invited scholars from all over Italy to live and teach in Rome. J. H. Plumb writes: "Philosophers, rhetoricians, poets, historians, philologists, grammarians, and teachers of Latin and Greek all were welcome in the new palace of the Vatican that Nicholas was creating."[41]

Other Renaissance popes followed in Nicholas's footsteps. Pius II (1458–1464),

Renaissance popes restored much of the splendor of Rome (pictured). Florence, however, remained unrivaled in grandeur and beauty.

a patron of classical studies, continued the rebuilding of Rome, as did Paul II (1464–1471). Sixtus IV, whose goal was that Rome should rival Florence as a cultural capital, brought many of Nicholas's unfinished projects to completion. Under Sixtus the famous Sistine Chapel, whose ceiling Michelangelo would later paint, was built. Sixtus also improved the Roman port, repaired ancient Roman aqueducts so they could once again carry water to the city, and fortified the outer defenses of Rome. He added a thousand more books to the library begun by Nicholas, commissioning the building of a new classical-style library to house the growing collection.

The popes were not alone in restoring the city's grandeur. The church drew its cardinals and other officials from some of the most wealthy and powerful families in Italy and Europe. These men, used to a life of luxury and always equating opulence with power, built palaces on a grand scale. Cardinals Rodrigo Borgia (Alexander VI), Pietro Barbo (Paul II), and their contemporaries built magnificent residences, large enough to accommodate more than two hundred servants, since a cardinal's household could include chamberlains, grooms, butchers, tailors, cooks, notaries, and numerous other functionaries.

Nevertheless, with all the building done by the popes and their cardinals, Rome had a long way to go to rival Florence. As the fifteenth century came to an end, the city still had not achieved undisputed greatness. Historian Peter Partner writes: "For all its echoes of the Empire of the Caesars, for all the clerical pageantry of its priestly residents, Rome was only a large, medieval village, smelling of cows and hay."[42]

The Turkish Threat

Various political problems conspired to draw the popes' attention away from rebuilding Rome. Important among these was a new threat of invasion from the East. In 1453 Constantinople fell to the Ottoman Turks, and the Eastern army threatened Italy. By 1456 it had captured the Greek city of Athens, and within a few years all of Greece was under the control of the Turks. One after the other, Serbia, Bosnia, Herzegovina, and Albania, which lay between Constantinople and Italy, fell to the Eastern army, and the Muslims entered into a struggle with Venice for control of the lucrative Adriatic trade routes.

In response to the Turkish threat Nicholas summoned all Christian rulers in Europe to mount a crusade. A unified assault on the Turks, however, never materialized. The northern European countries, preoccupied with nation building, refused their support.

Nicholas V's efforts to launch a crusade proved more successful in uniting Italy. He called upon the warring Italian city-states to make peace in the face of the Turkish threat. The first fruit of this effort was the Peace of Lodi, a 1454 treaty between Milan and Venice, traditional rivals for wealth and power in northern Italy. Within a year after the fall of Constantinople, other ma-

---

The Turkish Threat

From the fall of Constantinople in 1453, Renaissance popes made repeated calls for a new crusade. In 1459 Pope Pius II called a crusade congress to which very few leaders came. His response, recorded in his Commentaries, *translated by Florence Alden Gragg, demonstrates his displeasure.*

"Our Brethren and our sons, we hoped on arriving at this city [Mantua] to find that a throng of royal ambassadors had preceded us. We see that only a few are here. We have been mistaken. Christians are not so concerned about religion as we believed. We fixed the day for the Congress very far ahead. No one can say the time was too short; no one can plead the difficulties of travel. We who are old and ill have defied the Apennines and winter. . . . Not without danger we left the patrimony of the Church to come to the rescue of the Catholic faith which the Turks are doing their utmost to destroy. We saw their power increasing every day, their armies, which had already occupied Greece . . . over-running Hungary. . . . We feared (and this will surely happen if we do not take care) that once the Hungarians were conquered the Germans, Italians, and indeed all Europe would be subdued, a calamity that must bring with it the destruction of our Faith. We took thought to avert this evil; we called a Congress in this place; we summoned princes and peoples that we might together take counsel to defend Christendom. We came full of hope and we grieve to find it vain."

jor cities and city-states began to follow in the footsteps of Milan and Venice, forming the Italian League. Florence joined in August 1454, the Papal States in November, and Naples in January 1455.

Members of the league promised to not wage war on one another for twenty-five years and to support one another in case of outside attack. In addition, certain members, such as Venice, Milan, and Naples, were to keep standing armies that would discourage invasion from outside. Though the league did not absolutely keep the peace in Italy, much of the fighting among the city-states ceased, allowing the popes to focus some of their attention on the menace from the East. As it turned out, however, the more dangerous threat came from Italy's European neighbors.

The French Invasions of Italy

The Turkish threat threw Italy into decades of turmoil. Though the Ottomans did not invade, they provided the excuse for other armies to march on Italian territories. In 1494, claiming he was coming to fight the Turks, Charles VIII, king of France, descended on Italy.

For Charles there were good reasons to invade Italy. He believed he held some hereditary claim, through his great-grandfather, to the kingdom of Naples, and used that, along with the gathering of the Turks, as an excuse to march south. Because Italy was not a unified country, and the city-states were often at odds and in jealous competition, he assumed it would be easy to conquer the territories. Accordingly, in the autumn of 1494 Charles and the French army crossed the Alps and invaded Italy. Milan and the Papal States, who supported Charles, remained relatively unscathed as French troops passed through their domains. Florence, however, capitulated to the French, and Charles helped the Florentines depose the Medici and set up a new government headed by Girolamo Savonarola, a reformist monk. Leaving Florence in the hands of Savonarola, Charles marched south to Naples, which at the end of the fifteenth century was under the rule of King Alfonso II, a noble from the Spanish region of Aragon. Alfonso and his son Ferrantino fled before the French army, and Charles took possession of the kingdom without a fight.

The French king and his army, however, did not last long in the south. The people of Naples, angry that the French were seizing property and assuming government positions, rioted against the occupying army. Charles withdrew and began the long march back to his own country, where he died in 1498. Alfonso, with the support of Aragon and Castile, another Spanish region, returned to power in Naples.

Though Charles's occupation was short, it heightened French interest in Italy. In 1499 Charles's successor, Louis XII, launched another attack. Louis's goal was to gain possession of Milan. Against this threat, Italian alliances shifted swiftly. Naples, which had been Milan's enemy in the first invasion, agreed to support Milan in keeping the French out of Italy. Florence and the Papal States allied with France. Previously neutral Venice, a jealous rival of Milan, agreed to help Louis.

In August Louis took control of the duchy and Ludovico, head of Milan, fled

An Invitation to Invade

In 1494 Charles VIII invaded Italy, at the invitation of the Italians themselves. A Frenchman, Philip of Commines, in his Memoirs, *quoted in James Harvey Robinson's* Readings in European History, *describes this invitation.*

"In the year of 1493, the lord Ludovico [Sforza of Milan] began to solicit King Charles VIII, then reigning in France, to undertake an expedition into Italy, to conquer the kingdom of Naples, and to supplant and exterminate those who possessed it. . . . This Ludovico was a wise man, but very timorous and humble where he was in awe of any one, and false and deceitful when it was for his advantage; and this I do not speak by hearsay, but as one that knew him well, and had many transactions with him. But to proceed: In the year of 1493 he began to tickle King Charles, who was but twenty-two years of age, with the vanities and glories of Italy, demonstrating (as is reported) the right which he had to the fine kingdom of Naples. . . . [Tempted, our King, then] requested the Venetians to give him their assistance and counsel in his expedition, and they returned this answer: That he should be very welcome in Italy . . . [and though they could offer no direct support], they would rather assist than disturb him in his designs. . . . On the 23rd of August, 1494, [the King, therefore] set out from Vienne, and marched straight toward Asti."

In 1494 King Charles VIII of France launched an attack on Italy. Although the occupation was brief, it fueled French interest in the region.

Ambitious to gain new territory, Louis XII followed Charles's lead and descended into Italy in 1499.

to Austria, where he stayed for six months, raising an army to recapture his homeland. His attack on Louis, however, was a disaster. Ludovico was captured and imprisoned in France, where he died in 1508.

In August 1515 Francis I, Louis's successor, defeated the defending army in Milan and became its duke. He then set his sights on the Papal States, but rather than fighting, he negotiated with the pope, and gained the Italian cities of Parma and Piacenza, which had come into the pope's hands.

By 1516 all of northern Italy was directly or indirectly under the control of the French. In the south, Naples was still under Spanish rule. In central Italy, the Papal States were under the control of Medici pope Leo X, the son of Lorenzo the Magnificent.

The Return of the Medici

The Medici were also back in control in Florence. Savonarola had been executed in 1498, and following his death the Medici made another bid for power. Supported by the Spanish and the pope, they returned to their city. Giuliano de' Medici took control with the help of the Spanish infantry. When Giuliano died in 1516, Piero's son Lorenzo took over the city.

Fear and Love

In the early sixteenth century Niccolo Machiavelli wrote The Prince, *which he hoped would become a "how-to" book for Florentine rulers. Having lived through the early Renaissance, his ideas often seem cynical, as is the case with his following words on how a ruler should wish to be seen by his subjects.*

"I hold that it is much more secure to be feared than to be loved. . . . The reason for my answer is that one must say of men generally that they are ungrateful, mutable, pretenders and dissemblers, prone to avoid danger, thirsty for gain. So long as you benefit them they are all yours. . . . They offer you their blood, their property, their lives, their children, when the need for such things is remote. But when need comes upon you, they turn around. So if a prince has relied wholly on their words and is lacking in other preparations, he falls. . . . Men hesitate less to injure a man who makes himself loved than to injure one who makes himself feared, for their love is held by a chain of obligation, which, because of men's wickedness, is broken on every occasion for the sake of selfish profit; but their fear is secured by a dread of punishment which never fails you."

Niccolo Machiavelli is perhaps best known for his book The Prince.

Lorenzo, duke of Urbino, unlike his grandfather, Lorenzo the Magnificent, was not content to rule Florence unofficially. He ruled openly and controlled many aspects of Florentine life. Under Lorenzo, historian J. R. Hale writes:

The family intervened even in private lawsuits to obtain verdicts for pro-Mediceans. Steps were taken to exclude visiting preachers who by adopting the style of Savonarola might bring to mind his message. To be overheard speaking against the Medici was to run the risk of exile.[43]

It was to Lorenzo, duke of Urbino, that Niccolo Machiavelli dedicated his famous book *The Prince,* written in 1513. The book and the writer were both products of the cynicism that followed the French invasions of Italy.

Machiavelli

Born in 1469, the young Niccolo had grown up during the reign of Lorenzo the Magnificent, and had seen the benefits of a strong ruler. He had also lived to see how a strong government could be destroyed through incompetence. As a student of the humanities, he looked to the past to discover what traits a ruler needed to keep a government strong and intact, so that it could benefit those who lived under it. Through careful, though somewhat skewed, analysis of ancient and contemporary Italian history, he determined that only a ruthless dictator could provide the stability needed to bring security to his city-state. For Machiavelli the end—a secure, well-run state—justified the means, which could be honest or corrupt, generous or greedy, cruel or kindly, depending on what would most strengthen the prince. Among other things, he wrote that it was more important for a ruler to be feared than loved and more important to appear virtuous than to be virtuous. This was a distinct break from traditional humanist thought, a fact which Machiavelli realized but nonetheless deemed necessary. In *The Prince,* he wrote:

> I break away completely from principles laid down by my predecessors. But since it is my purpose to write something useful to an attentive reader, I think it more effective to go back to the practical truth of the subject. . . .

Machiavelli dedicated The Prince *to Lorenzo, duke of Urbino (pictured), who, like Machiavelli, believed in the benefits of a strong ruler.*

> For there is such a difference between the way men live and the way they ought to live.[44]

The High Renaissance, of which Machiavelli was a part, was a time of struggle and strife in Italy. The greed and jealousy the Italian city-states had felt for one another had brought invaders to the peninsula. The innocence and sparkle which had characterized the learning and cultural blossoming of the early Renaissance was exchanged for a view of life that was practical but lacked the ideals of virtue, communal rule, and heroism. Humanism evolved into secularism as popes and princes alike sought power and wealth.

6 Three Great Artists of the High Renaissance

At the turn of the sixteenth century, Italy, mired in war, intrigue, and deception, was nevertheless the spot of one of the most concentrated and creative cultural flowerings in the history of art. From the workshops of Rome and Florence to the court of Milan, Italian artists created paintings and sculptures that would be held up as standards of excellence for centuries to come. In the first part of the sixteenth century, three of the most famous artists in history—Leonardo da Vinci (1452–1519), Michelangelo Buonarroti (1475–1564), and Raphael Santi (1483–1520)—were living and working in Italy.

That three such geniuses should be alive and creating at the same time in the same part of the world has intrigued many modern-day scholars and art historians. E. H. Gombrich writes:

> One may well ask why it was that all these great masters were born in the same time period, but such questions are more easily asked than answered. One cannot explain the existence of genius.[45]

Several relevant facts contributed to the likelihood of these artists' successes. The discoveries and innovations of the artists of the Trecento and Quattrocento set the stage for the artists of the Cinquecento (the 1500s). With the pioneering work of Giotto, Brunelleschi, Masaccio, and others, the use of perspective, foreshortening, and modeling, along with other techniques, had been introduced to Renaissance artists. By the time of Leonardo, Michelangelo, and Raphael, many artists were masters of these techniques, willing to pass them along to the younger artists who worked as apprentices in their shops.

The tradition of innovation and discovery was especially strong in Florence, where all three artists learned or practiced their craft. Leonardo was apprenticed to the Florentine painter and sculptor Andrea del Verrocchio. Michelangelo worked under the tutelage of the Florentine painter Domenico Ghirlandaio. Raphael, the youngest of the artists, before moving to Florence studied in Umbria under the master Pietro Perugino, who himself had been trained in Florence by Verrocchio.

In addition, in Florence especially, the wealthy displayed their power by commissioning grand works of art. Dukes, kings, popes, and others competed with one another for honor and prestige. Gombrich explains:

> To erect magnificent buildings, to commission splendid tombs, to order

great cycles of frescoes, or to dedicate a painting for the high altar of a famous church was considered a sure way of perpetuating one's name and securing a worthy monument to one's earthly existence.[46]

Good artists were, therefore, in great demand. With so many patrons competing for their work, artists commanded more freedom and a stronger social position. Often the best artists could be quite selective in accepting commissions, choosing those allowing them greater creative control over the work. Whereas in the past men like Lorenzo de' Medici could dictate the details of an artist's work, the artists of the Cinquecento could more often follow their own creative impulses. They enjoyed an unprecedented amount of freedom to experiment.

Leonardo da Vinci

Experimentation was at the heart of all Leonardo did. He believed that painting was a science based on both the study of nature and the study of mathematical perspective. He therefore studied and experimented in zoology, botany, geology, anatomy, optics, and more. His notebooks are filled with scientific observations of the world and with sketches drawn from nature.

Anatomy he considered especially important, and he performed dissections on

The drawings of Leonardo da Vinci reveal his great intellect and fascination with the study of nature. Clearly, Leonardo embodied the spirit of learning that characterized the Renaissance.

 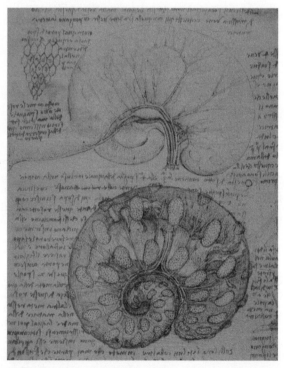

Leonardo's fresco The Last Supper *is noted for depicting a variety of emotions and gestures. It remains one of the most famous works of Renaissance art.*

both human and animal cadavers to learn exactly how the muscles and internal organs worked so he could paint human and animal forms more accurately. His detailed sketches added much to Renaissance knowledge of anatomy. For example, his sketch *Embryo in the Womb*, though it contains some inaccuracies, is so true to life Helen Gardner says it could be used in modern medical instruction.

Leonardo's study of nature also included psychology, which he believed should be reflected in painting. He wrote:

> A good painter has two chief objects to paint—man and the intention of his soul. The former is easy, the latter hard, for it must be expressed by gestures and the movement of the limbs.[47]

Leonardo's ability to capture the intention of his painted figure's soul is ap-

parent in his work *The Last Supper*. Leonardo chose to paint the scene at the point in time immediately following Jesus' words "one of you will betray me." The disciples react with varying emotions, as they ask themselves and one another (according to biblical tradition), "Is it I?"

In Leonardo's painting, each disciple displays, through body posture and facial expression, an individual response to Jesus' statement. Together, their emotions create dramatic tension as they turn to one another in love, rage, doubt, fear, and denial. Jesus, however, sits placidly in the center of the painting, isolated and framed by a doorway whose arch acts as a halo. Jesus' forehead is the intersecting point of all the perspective lines, drawing the viewer to focus still more on him. This central placement and Jesus' peaceful demeanor work together to make him the

The Psychology of Painting

Among many subjects Leonardo da Vinci studied, psychology drew his attention as he tried to figure out how the intentions of a person could be manifested in painting. In "Of How to Represent Some One Who Is Speaking Among a Group of Persons," in his private notebook, he wrote:

"When you desire to represent anyone speaking among a group of persons you ought to consider first the subject of which he has to treat, and how so to order his actions that they may be in keeping with this subject. That is, if the subject be persuasive the actions should serve the intention; if it be one that needs to be expounded under various heads, the speaker should take a finger of his left hand between two fingers of his right, keeping the two smaller ones closed, and then let his face be animated and turned towards the people, with mouth slightly opened, so as to give the effect of speaking. And if he is seated let him seem to be in the act of raising himself more upright, with his head forward; and if you represent him standing, make him leaning forward a little with head and shoulders towards the populace, whom you should show silent and attentive, and all watching the face of the orator with gestures of admiration."

most important figure in the painting. Leonardo combined geometrical expertise and psychological understanding to give added meaning to this scene from the Bible.

Another of his most famous paintings, the *Mona Lisa*, demonstrates his interest in optics. For nearly five centuries art critics have discussed the "mysterious" qualities of this portrait. The woman in the painting has been described as sad, wise, mocking, peaceful, and even seductive. She seems to be alive and change according to the personality of the individual who is viewing her. This "mysterious" quality is no accident. It is a result of Leonardo's understanding of how viewers perceive what they see.

Leonardo discovered that to bring life to a painting the artist needed to leave something to the imagination of the person viewing the work. From his study of optics, he knew that the eye would fill in what the painter left out. When he painted the mouth and eyes of the *Mona Lisa*, therefore, he blurred the lines at their edges, letting them fade into shadow. Because the lines are not definite, the expression on the face of the *Mona Lisa* seems, to the viewer, to be elusive and changeable. The effect is a product of the artist's knowledge of nature and skill in painting.

However, Leonardo was not only in demand as a great painter. He was also an inventor interested in military engineering, hydraulics, and mechanics. In a world in which empire building and war were primary occupations, many prosperous patrons of the time were attracted to Leonardo's engineering capabilities. He worked as a military engineer for the duke of Milan, Cesare Borgia, and the French king Francis I. In a letter to the duke of Milan, he stressed the arts of war over the arts of peace:

I have methods of destroying every rock or other fortress, even if it were

Even today viewers continue to ponder the elusive and mysterious Mona Lisa, *painted by Leonardo about 1514.*

founded on a rock. . . . If the fight should be at sea I have kinds of machines most efficient for offence and defense. . . . I will make covered chariots, safe and unattackable. . . . In case of need I will make big guns, mortars and light ordinance.[48]

With so many interests competing for attention in his lively mind, Leonardo completed very few of his paintings. Thus, as Gardner writes: "We still look with awe on his achievements and, even more, on his unfulfilled promise."[49]

Michelangelo Buonarroti

If Leonardo left the promise of his genius unfulfilled, Michelangelo brought the promise of humanist art to fruition. A sculptor, painter, architect, poet, and engineer, Michelangelo, like Leonardo, was a man of prodigious ability. More than any other artist who came before him, he had faith in his own genius and followed his own vision. He believed that the artist made the Ideal come to life in his work. This meant that rather than imitating the world around him, the artist, especially the sculptor, revealed higher truths, which lay hidden in nature. His works idealize the natural world, most especially the human form.

With this philosophy, he created some of the most dramatic and best-loved sculptures in the history of art. His *David, Moses, Dying Slave,* and *Bound Slave* are still considered the height of genius. All sculpted from marble, these works are of dramatic proportion, dynamic in tension. Each reveals the inner psychology of the subject. Above all, they glory

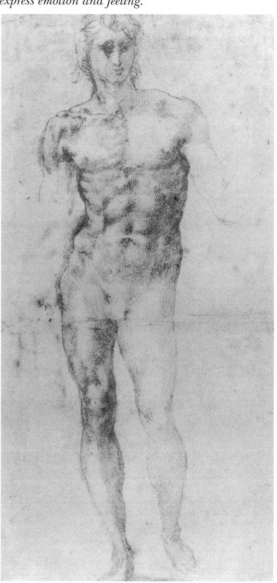

in the human form, which Michelangelo learned to depict in more varied postures of repose and movement than any other artist before him.

Unfortunately, Michelangelo's irritable personality was almost as famous as his art. He strongly disliked Leonardo, he was jealous of Raphael, and he fought with many of his patrons. His most famous battle of wills was with the powerful and bad-tempered Pope Julius II.

In 1503 Julius succeeded Pius III to the throne of Saint Peter. Julius was a warrior and an empire builder. His three main goals during his papacy were to drive the French out of Italy, establish the Papal States as a powerful political entity, and make Rome the most grand and beautiful city in the world. For this last goal, he desperately needed the help of the best sculptors, painters, and architects in Italy.

In 1505 Julius called Michelangelo to Rome to work on a great tomb that would immortalize him and his papacy. Before Michelangelo could begin work, however, the pope halted the project. Michelangelo, who had already spent six months picking out marble for the tomb, was angry and felt betrayed, imagining also that rival artists were contriving against him, and even

Michelangelo brought marble to life with the creation of masterpieces such as David *(left) and* Dying Slave *(right).*

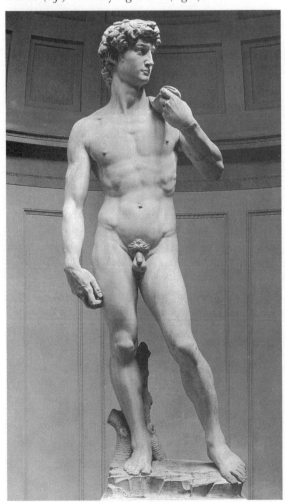

suspecting one of trying to poison him. Angry and fearful, he left Rome for Florence. From Florence he wrote a rude letter to the pope, saying that if Julius wanted him, he could come looking for him.

Rather than bringing the wrath of the pope down on the artist's head, this audacious letter sent Julius and Florentine officials into a flurry of negotiations. The Florentines, afraid Julius would take his anger out on them, worked to persuade Michelangelo to reconcile with the pope. This the artist eventually did with dramatic flair. Biographer Robert N. Linscott describes the meeting between Julius and Michelangelo:

> Michelangelo met the Pope at Bologna and threw himself at his feet with a

noose about his neck in token of submission. A bishop who was present attempted to intercede, saying that artists were ignorant creatures who knew no better, whereupon the terrible-tempered Pope beat the bishop with his staff, crying out, "It is you who are ignorant."[50]

Michelangelo returned to Rome, where he went to work on his most famous project—the ceiling of the Sistine Chapel. In four short years, working with only two assistants, who mixed his pigments and helped him transfer his designs onto plaster, the painter covered 5,800 square feet of ceiling with more than three hundred figures. These figures, each a work of art, weave together to tell the story of the cre-

---

The Art of War

Leonardo da Vinci was a master not only of art, but of science and engineering as well. In a letter to the duke of Milan, written in 1493, quoted in A Documentary History of Art, *he lists a number of ways he could help the duke in times of war.*

"(1) I have a sort of extremely light and strong bridges, adapted to be most easily carried, and with them you may pursue, and at any time flee from the enemy; and others, secure and indestructible by fire and battle, easy and convenient to lift and place. Also method of burning and destroying those of the enemy. . . .

(3). . . If by reason of the height of the banks, or the strength of the place and its position, it is impossible, when besieging a place, to avail oneself of the plan of bombardment, I have methods of destroying every rock or other fortress, even if it were founded on a rock, etc.

(4) Again, I have kinds of mortars; most convenient and easy to carry; and with these I can fling small stones almost resembling a storm; and with the smoke of these cause great terror to the enemy, to his great detriment and confusion."

Michelangelo's frescoes on the ceiling of the Sistine Chapel rank among the greatest achievements in the history of art. The Creation of Adam *is one of the most famous scenes.*

ation, fall, and redemption of man in the Christian tradition.

The ceiling is also a stunning example of a merging of the classical and Christian traditions in a work of art. Pagan sibyls, Hebrew prophets, and the ancestors of Christ all share space in this monumental work. In one of the most famous scenes, *The Creation of Adam,* man and God are linked by a spark of divine energy. Both are of mythic proportions and both seem to be made of flesh. The first man is created in the image of God, and his nude body is idealized—a true reflection of heavenly perfection. Woman, too, has a role in this scene of creation. Under God's arm is a figure that some believe is Eve and others believe is Jesus' mother, Mary. As yet uncreated, she watches the creation of Adam.

Throughout the painting of the ceiling, Michelangelo and the pope bickered. Julius accused Michelangelo of taking too long and Michelangelo called the pope unreasonable. At one point Michelangelo informed Julius that the work would be done "when it satisfies me in its artistic details."[51] Julius responded that if the project was not finished immediately he would have the artist thrown into the scaffolding. Michelangelo believed the pope's threat, dismantled the scaffolding, and called the project done.

Raphael Santi

Unlike Michelangelo, Raphael was known far and wide for his sweet personality. He was said to be friendly, courteous, and gifted with the ability to unify and pacify those who worked with him. Vasari says Raphael "was so full of nobility and kindness that even the animals loved him."[52]

This mildness of temper and sweetness of personality are reflected in Raphael's work, which he painted in the calm, balanced, ordered style of the classical Greeks. Serenity, dignity, sweetness, and idealism are reflected in the many Madonnas he painted during his short career. As a humanist, he painted the mother of God in a style that reflected both deep Christian devotion and a worldly love of beauty. As a result, these portraits of Mary remain unrivaled in the history of art.

Raphael's expertise and genial temper soon drew the attention of Pope Julius, who called Raphael to Rome in 1508. There he received one of the largest commissions of the time, the painting of the papal apartments in the Vatican. The first

Raphael's mild disposition and love of beauty are reflected in the soft lines and delicate color of his famous Madonna pictures. Pictured are Raphael's Madonna of the Goldfinch *(right) and the* Madonna of the Cloth *(left).*

room of the apartments he devoted to the four branches of human knowledge—theology, law, poetry, and philosophy. Most likely under the guidance of Julius's classical scholars, he focused on the ideals of wisdom, knowledge, and virtue, which he felt would be appropriate study for the pope.

Julius was not Raphael's only papal patron. Leo X, son of Lorenzo de' Medici, who succeeded Julius in 1513, also commissioned works by Raphael. A true Medici, Leo was a worldly connoisseur of the arts and his love of opulence brought Rome a splendid pageantry that it had not seen since ancient times. In Leo's court Raphael's prestige increased. Wealthy, handsome, and with his sweet personality, he charmed the court of Leo, Rome, and all of Italy.

Unfortunately, Raphael died in 1520 at the young age of thirty-seven. Leonardo had died the year before. Only Michelan-

Raphael charmed Pope Leo X, who commissioned many works of art. This picture of Pope Leo X was painted by Raphael (top). (Right) One of his greatest works, Raphael's School of Athens *shows his interest in classical culture. The fresco portrays ancient Greek scientists and philosophers.*

High Commendation

The artist Raphael was known far and wide for his beautiful paintings and his sweet personality. This letter of recommendation, written by Duchess Giovanna to the gonfalonier *of Florence in 1504, reprinted in* The Raphael Book, *recounts his good qualities.*

"Most magnificent and powerful seignior, whom I must honor as a father. . . . He who will present this letter to you, Raphael, painter of Urbino, gifted with a fine talent in his art, has decided to pass some time at Florence to perfect himself in his studies. As his father, who was dear to me, was full of good qualities, so is the son a young man of modest and distinguished manners, and therefore, I cherish him on every account and wish him to attain perfection. This is why I recommend him, as much and as earnestly as I can, to your highness, with entreaty that it may please you for love of me to accord him aid and protection at every opportunity. I shall regard as rendered to myself and as an agreeable token of friendship to me, every service and every kindness which he shall receive from your lordship. . . . Joanna Feltria de Ruvere, Duchess of Sora, and Wife of the Prefect of Rome."

gelo survived the passing of the Italian High Renaissance. In a sonnet written in 1554, ten years before his death, Michelangelo talks about his life. His poem may be said to describe the Renaissance and its decline:

> The course of my long life hath reached at last,
> In fragile bark o'er a tempestuous sea,
> The common harbor where must rendered be
> Account of all actions of the past.
>
> The impassioned phantasy, that vague and vast,
> Made art an idol and a king to me,

> Was an illusion, and but vanity
> Were the desires that lured me and harassed.
>
> The dreams of love, that were so sweet of yore,
> What are they now, when two deaths may be mine,
> One sure, and one forecasting its alarms?
>
> Painting and sculpture satisfy no more.
> The soul now turning to the Love Divine,
> That oped, to embrace us, on the cross its arms.[53]

Chapter

7 The Late Renaissance

Sixteenth-century Italians witnessed the passing of the Renaissance. Even while Leonardo, Michelangelo, and Raphael were working in Rome, Milan, and Florence, destructive currents could be detected in northern Europe. Such seemingly diverse and remote events as the exploration of the New World and the disaffection of the working classes in northern Europe were creating changes that would undermine, then overtake, the Renaissance in Italy.

Because of their explorations in the New World, the Spanish challenged Italy in the area of trade. Following Christopher Columbus's historic 1492 voyage, Spain claimed territory in the vast and rich Americas. Cargoes from the New World included silver, sugar, dyes, vanilla, cacao, and cotton. Portuguese explorers

Columbus's exploration of the New World heralded changes that indirectly brought an end to the Renaissance.

such as Bartholomew Dias and Vasco da Gama discovered new trade routes to the East, opening the markets of Africa and India to the Portuguese. Spices, sugar, dyes, precious stones, silk, alum, ivory, and other luxury goods from the East poured into Europe through the Portuguese port of Lisbon. Spain and Portugal soon equaled, then replaced, the Italian city-states as centers of trade.

With this influx of riches, Europe on the whole prospered. The new wealth encouraged the expansion of manufacturing. Printing, mining, shipping, weapons, and textile industries grew on the continent. Families who had traditionally been in the banking business, such as the Medici in Italy and their rivals in northern Europe, grew richer.

Watching the growth of affluence in their society, the poor and working classes had high expectations of prosperity for themselves. Contrary to these expectations, however, they did not share in the wealth. During the sixteenth century, inflation rose at an average of 2 percent a year. Prices doubled in Spain by the middle of the century and in Germany the cost of food and clothing increased 100 percent between 1519 and 1540. The wages of workers did not rise in proportion to inflation and the gap between rich

---

Speaking in Unknown Tongues

At the turn of the sixteenth century, reformers found much to criticize in the Catholic Church. Erasmus of Rotterdam, in notes he wrote on the New Testament, quoted in James Anthony Froude's The Life and Letters of Erasmus, *takes issue with church ceremony, which he believed overshadowed the teachings in the Bible.*

"St. Paul says he would rather speak five words with a reasonable meaning in them than ten thousand in an unknown tongue. They chant nowadays in our churches in what is an unknown tongue and nothing else, while you will not hear a sermon once in six months telling people to amend their lives. Modern church music is so constructed that the congregation cannot hear one distinct word. The choristers themselves do not understand what they are singing, yet according to priests and monks it constitutes the whole of religion. Why will they not listen to St. Paul? In college or monastery it is still the same: music nothing but music. There was no music in St. Paul's time. Words were then pronounced plainly. Words nowadays mean nothing. They are mere sounds striking upon the ear, and men are to leave their work and go to church to listen to worse noises than were ever heard in Greek or Roman theatre. . . . If they want music let them [choir boys] sing Psalms like rational beings, and not too many of those."

and poor widened. In addition, those who had money charged high interest on loans. The result was class conflict. Donald Kagan argues:

> This [disparity between rich and poor] greatly aggravated the traditional social divisions between the clergy and the laity, the higher and the lower clergy, the urban patricate and the guilds, masters and journeymen, and the landed nobility and the agrarian peasantry.[54]

Kagan believes this tension between the classes may have indirectly paved the way for the end of the Renaissance. Dissatisfied and wanting more, the poor and working classes grew critical of traditional ruling institutions. They became more open to ideas that would accelerate change and bring them a greater degree of freedom, wealth, and equality. These ideals were embodied in a reform movement fomenting in northern Europe. The target of this movement was the Catholic Church.

The Papacy in Trouble

The popes of the High Renaissance were empire builders, preoccupied with military, political, and worldly concerns. They reasoned that if the church was ever to recover from the negative effects of the Avignon Papacy and the Great Schism, Rome had to reestablish itself as the center of European Christianity. This resulted in increasing military action, political maneuvering, and in the glorification of the Eternal City, all of which required that the popes increase their revenues and consolidate their power.

Nepotism continued into the late Renaissance. Simony, the practice of selling important church offices regardless of the qualifications of the buyer, created even more problems. Many church officials who purchased offices lived in Rome, far away from the areas they governed. The Germans, especially, resented nonresident clergy who milked local people for taxes and had no sympathy with their problems. Between 1450 and 1515 the Germans held at least a hundred district councils, as well as four provincial ones, to call for an end to simony and the appointments of unsuitable bishops. Their calls for reform, however, had no effect.

The sale of indulgences also caused dissatisfaction. Indulgences were pieces of paper that insured buyers they were forgiven of their sins and would not, at death, go to purgatory. Instead of doing penance, performing good works to atone for their sins, they could simply buy an indulgence. In the early sixteenth century indulgences had been expanded to cover any future sins a person might commit and could also be purchased on behalf of dead relatives who might be suffering in purgatory. In effect, people felt they could buy their way into heaven.

This belief was quite often encouraged by the church because money from the sale of indulgences was a good source of income. Proceeds from indulgence sales went to pay for church projects, such as the construction of magnificent buildings in Rome. Money was also used to help high church officials get out of debt. For example, one archbishop of Germany, Albrecht, finding himself deeply in debt, joined with a German banking house and Pope Leo X to sell indulgences. Half the money from the sales went to the pope in

Rome and the other half to Albrecht and his creditors.

Because the sale of indulgences was an important source of income for Rome and its representatives, "indulgence preachers" went to great lengths to frighten potential buyers into purchases. Often they played on the fears and guilt of their audiences, as did John Tetzel, who worked on the Albrecht project. In one indulgence sermon, Tetzel is quoted as exhorting his listeners:

Don't you hear the voices of your dead parents and other relatives crying out, "Have mercy on us, for we suffer great punishment and pain. From this you could release us with a few alms. . . . We have created you, fed you, cared for you, and left you our temporal goods. Why do you treat us so cruelly and leave us to suffer in the flames when it takes only a little to save us?[55]

Martin Luther

The sale of indulgences in general and the tactics of men like Tetzel in particular angered Martin Luther, a German priest. A thoughtful young man, Luther had observed the problems in his church and decided change was needed. In addition to opposing nepotism, simony, and indulgences, he also believed faith should be based on the Bible and not on the non-biblical writings of popes and other church scholars. He concluded that faith in Christ alone, not religious works or participation in ceremonies, led to righteousness and salvation. Good works and money could not buy the forgiveness of sins.

Shocked by the debauchery of the Catholic Church, Martin Luther campaigned for reform, fueling a period of religious and political upheaval across Europe.

Luther began his campaign for reform by writing letters to local bishops, describing what he felt were the problems in the church. When he was disappointed by their answers, tradition says he posted a list of his complaints, known as the Ninety-five Theses, on the door of the Castle Church at Wittenberg in Germany. Many of them had to do with indulgences, as is evident in the first four theses. Luther wrote:

1. Our Lord and Master Christ, in saying "Do penance," intended the whole life of every man to be penance.

2. This word cannot be understood as referring to penance as a sacrament

(that is, confession and satisfaction, as by the ministry of priests).

3. This word also does not refer solely to inner penitence; indeed there is no penitence unless it produces various outward mortifications of the flesh.

4. Therefore punishment [of sin] remains as long as the hatred of self (that is, true inward penitence), namely until entering the kingdom of heaven.[56]

Luther was not the only person calling for church reform. In Switzerland, Denmark, Sweden, Poland, France, England, and elsewhere in Europe, various groups supported, and often fought for, change. Even in Rome itself, a group of priests and laymen called the Oratory of Divine Love argued for church reform.

The Sack of Rome

While the call for reform was spreading across Europe, the papacy was running afoul of the northern monarchs. In 1519 Holy Roman Emperor Maximilian I died. Both Francis I of France and Charles I of Spain vied to become the new emperor. Pope Leo X backed the French, but Charles won the day to become Emperor Charles V.

As Holy Roman Emperor, Charles inherited a vast empire that included Spain, his homeland, the Netherlands, Austria, Sardinia, Sicily, Naples, Milan, and other smaller parts of central Europe. The French, who had many quarrels with Spain, disputed Charles's Italian holdings.

Francis I of France (left) and Charles I of Spain vied for the title of Holy Roman Emperor. Although Pope Leo X favored the French, Charles was crowned Emperor Charles V (right).

Spain and France went to war, and Italy was one of their battlegrounds.

Clement VII, who was pope from 1523 to 1534, feared that Charles would try to add Florence and the Papal States to his empire. He decided to side with France. By the winter of 1526–1527, however, the imperial army was camped near Bologna in the Papal States.

Losing faith in France's ability to protect him, the pope tried, too late, to call a truce with Charles. But the imperial army, whose pay was far in arrears, could not resist the temptation of the wealth of Rome.

Taking matters into their own hands, the imperial soldiers marched south.

On the morning of May 6, 1527, Charles's army, part German and part Spanish, invaded the Eternal City. The Germans, who were mostly Lutheran, showed their hatred of Rome and the pope. They looted churches and monasteries and beat, harassed, and murdered clergymen. They destroyed many of the manuscripts in the Vatican library and devastated many private libraries. They looted and burned palaces, and murdered or held the owners for ransom. Soldiers

A Letter to Pope Leo

Martin Luther, the Catholic priest who headed the reform movement in Germany, objected strenuously to what he considered the corruption of the papacy. In this letter to Leo X, reprinted in Will Durant's The Reformation, *he warns the pope not to be misled by wicked men in the church.*

"Thy reputation, and the fame of thy blameless life . . . are too well known and too high to be assailed. . . . But thy See, which is called the Roman Curia, and of which neither thou nor any man can deny that it is more corrupt than any Babylon or Sodom ever was, and which is, as far as I can see, characterized by a totally depraved, hopeless, and notorious wickedness—that See I have truly despised. . . . The Roman Church has become the most licentious den of thieves, the most shameless of all brothels, the kingdom of sin, death, and hell. . . . I have always grieved . . . that thou has been made pope in these times, for thou wert worthy of better days . . . .

Do not listen, therefore, my dear Leo, to those sirens who make thee out to be no mere man but a demigod. . . . Be not deceived by those who pretend that thou art lord of the world . . . who prate that thou has power over heaven, hell, and purgatory . . . for under cover of thy name they seek to set up their own wickedness in the Church, and, alas, through them Satan has already made much headway under thy predecessors."

The papacy of Clement VII was marked by struggles with Charles V, whom the pope feared would try to conquer Florence and the papal states.

raped Catholic nuns, pried open tombs, and robbed graves. In a frenzy of plunder, they stole religious relics, family treasures, and great works of Italian art. Makeshift markets, where soldiers sold and traded stolen goods, soon sprang up in the streets of Rome.

For seven months imperial soldiers occupied the sacked city. By the time they left, Rome was thoroughly demoralized. Following the initial looting, food shortages and disease claimed many lives. It is estimated that ten thousand citizens of Rome died during the occupation. An equal number fled before the Spanish and German occupation.

Though it drew much attention, Rome was not the only Italian city that was sacked in the first half of the sixteenth century. Invading armies also marched into Brescia, Genoa, and Pavia. Florence and Naples, though they were not plundered, suffered greatly from sieges. Much of Italy was in turmoil.

The Council of Trent

Though the city recovered, the sack of Rome and the European spread of the reform movement shook the papacy for decades. In 1545 Paul III, the last Renaissance pope, called church leaders to the Council of Trent. Their goal was to make long-needed reforms in the church. This council, which lasted long past Paul's papacy, met three times, in a process that spanned eighteen years. From 1545 to 1547, from 1551 to 1552, and from 1562 to 1563, church officials, who were mostly Italian, gathered to discuss the fate of their religion.

The reforms that came out of the Council of Trent were mostly concerned with internal discipline. Simony was curtailed. Bishops who lived in Rome were forced to move to their dioceses. Local bishops were granted more authority to monitor and discipline their parishioners. Local priests, in response to parishioner complaints, were required to be better educated, celibate, and, henceforth, neatly dressed.

The church made no doctrinal concessions, however. It maintained the traditional teachings of the popes and church scholars, and did not confirm that the Bible was the sole source of Christian belief. They retained the doctrine that good works played a role in the salvation of the

The Pomp of Rome

Many proponents of reform objected to the opulence and pageantry of Rome. The richness of the ceremonies and the participants indeed were splendid, as can be seen in this description of the arrival of the cardinals at the palace of Pope Paul III on Christmas Day 1547. William Thomas, a Welshman who was present, described the spectacle in his book The History of Italy.

"There was no cardinal that came without a great train of gentlemen and prelates, well horsed and appointed—some had forty, some fifty, and some sixty or more—and next before every of them rode two henchmen, the one carrying a cushion and a rich cloth, and the other a pillar of silver; and the cardinals themselves, appareled in robes of crimson . . . with red hats on their heads, rode on mules.

When they were all come to the palace . . . the Bishop [pope] himself, with the three-crowned miter full of jewels, in a very rich cope[full-length vestment], with shoes of crimson velvet set with precious stones, and in all his other pontifical apparel, came forth and at the chamber door sat him down in a chair of crimson velvet, through which runneth two staves covered with the same. Thus being set, the prelates and clergy with the other officers passed on afore him . . . all in scarlet and for the most part finely furred . . . and after that the cardinals by two and two, and between every two a great rout of gentlemen. Then came the ambassadors and next them the Bishop himself, blessing all the way and carried in his chair by eight men, clothed in long robes of scarlet."

soul, and continued the sale of indulgences. In these, and in all the other areas of doctrine that had been questioned, the teachings of the Catholic Church remained as they had been before the Reformation movement began.

From this time on, there was never again one Christian church in western Europe. There were Catholics in Italy, Spain, Ireland, and much of France, Austria, and Poland. Other countries and areas adopted various forms of Protestantism. Norway, Sweden, Denmark, and much of Germany were Lutheran. Most of England was Anglican. Scotland, the Netherlands, Switzerland, and small parts of France, England, Germany, and Poland were Calvinist. A united European Christian empire with Rome as its center never materialized. The Renaissance popes' dream had failed.

This failure, accompanied as it was with the turmoil of war and reform, could not help but affect the artists of the day.

Even before the sack of Rome, as early as 1520 High Renaissance art began to falter. While Michelangelo was still working in Rome, other artists were developing the Mannerist style, which at once emulated and negated the work of the great artists who had come before them.

Mannerism

Confronted with what they believed was the perfection of men like Leonardo, Michelangelo, and Raphael, these new artists fought desperately to develop a perfection and a style that would be unique to them. After all, Leonardo had once written: "Poor is the pupil who does not surpass his master."[57]

This was a monumental task for those who worked in the late Renaissance. Early Renaissance artists had overcome many technical problems in painting by observing nature and exploring scientific developments in optics. High Renaissance artists, armed with these new techniques, had worked at bringing art to life: Leonardo did this by minutely studying the natural world around him. Raphael idealized nature by painting scenes of beautiful proportion and serene order. Michelangelo went even further in transcending nature, creating perfect figures and subjects.

Many artists in the late Renaissance, believing perfection had been attained, abandoned nature as their model and turned to other works of art for inspiration. They especially devoted their attention to the great paintings and sculptures of Michelangelo and the ancient Romans. Nature, they felt, was rough compared with the perfection of art. They sought to find an ideal for art in other art, and to develop their own inventive manner of interpreting their subjects.

Mannerist painting, therefore, is highly stylized and self-involved. Unlike High Renaissance art, which found harmony in balance and proportion, Mannerist work is often unstable. Figures are distorted and exaggerated in bizarre postures in settings that seem ambiguous. For example, in his painting *Madonna with the Long Neck*, Parmigianino created an unsettling scene of Mary and the Christ child. In the foreground, a large Madonna with a long neck, oval head, and oversize hands is completely out of proportion with herself. Some parts of her body are too large and other parts are too small to be a copy of nature. She is also out of proportion with the rest of the painting. She is much larger than the angels who come to adore the newborn Christ child. Christ himself lies sprawled in her lap. Unlike the animated young savior of the High Renaissance, however, this child does not seem to hold the promise of future redemption. He appears ill or dead, dangling from his mother's arms.

In addition, the two sides of the painting do not match. The Madonna, child, and the figures assumed to be angels on the left side of the painting seem to be very close to the viewer. On the right side of the painting, in deep perspective, is a solitary man who seems to be in a distant place, out of contact with the adoration scene. It almost seems as if he could be in another painting. The whole effect is unsettling for the viewer.

Many art historians see this as an allegory for the state of the church during the Reformation. The Madonna, they claim, represents the church, out of proportion, self-involved, and affected. The Christ child represents Christianity, which has grown ill or died in the arms of the church. The man in the distance is the Christian who no longer has any contact with the large, unnatural church, which has killed his faith in religion.

Whether or not this reading is correct, it does seem to describe the state of the church during this tumultuous period. It is also in keeping with the cynicism and

Mannerism took root in the aftermath of the High Renaissance. Typical of Mannerist style, Parmigianino's Madonna with the Long Neck *shows human forms elongated and stretched out of proportion.*

overintellectualization that was part of the Mannerist style and that characterized much art until the end of the sixteenth century.

The Fate of Humanism

Just as art changed in the late Renaissance, humanism, which had been the cornerstone of Renaissance culture, changed to meet the needs of a new society. Many early reformers had received humanist educations. Desiderius Erasmus in the Netherlands, Martin Luther in Germany, and John Calvin in Switzerland, among others, had been trained in the classical liberal arts. Though many reformists objected to what they considered to be the secular and pagan aspects of humanism—the Italian obsession with aesthetics, grandeur, and the ancient non-Christian writers—they maintained the study of the liberal arts. An understanding of history, grammar, poetry, rhetoric, and languages, they reasoned, could aid in the study of religion and the Bible.

Liberal arts as a program of study was implemented in many Protestant schools and universities. At the University of Wittenberg, Philip Melanchthon, a professor of Greek, encouraged the humanist study of history and poetry, among the other liberal arts. Along with Martin Luther, Melanchthon insisted that both Hebrew and Greek be taught at Wittenberg. With such expertise, students could study and translate the Bible and the works of early Christians and compare them.

In Switzerland the founders of the Genevan Academy followed in Luther and Melanchthon's footsteps. Created primar-

A Perfect Lady

As the Renaissance progressed, the Italians became more and more enamored of rules. Baldassare Castiglione, in The Book of the Courtier, *written between 1513 and 1518, describes the proper behavior for a lady of good breeding.*

"I think, that in her ways, manners, words, gestures and bearing, a woman ought to be very unlike a man. . . . It is seemly for a woman to have a soft and delicate tenderness, with an air of womanly sweetness in her every movement. . . . In a Lady who lives at court a certain pleasing affability is becoming above all else, whereby she will be able to entertain graciously every kind of man with agreeable and comely conversation to the time and place and to the station of the person with whom she speaks. . . . As for bodily exercises, it is not seemly for a woman to handle weapons, ride, play tennis, wrestle and do many other things that are suited to men. . . . [She, however, should have] a knowledge of letters, of music, of painting and . . . how to be festive, adding a discreet modesty and the giving of a good impression of herself."

ily to train Calvinist ministers, the academy sent well-educated preachers to countries throughout Europe. Through these students, the study of the liberal arts was carried to France, Scotland, England, and, eventually, to the New World. In this way, humanist studies were kept alive during a period of intense change.

A Fading Away

Just as no one date signals the beginning of the Italian Renaissance, no one time or place can mark its end. Egalitarian humanism evolved into imperial humanism and then into theological humanism, becoming the handmaiden of a reformed church. The innocence of early Renaissance art erupted in the passion and drama of mature High Renaissance grandeur, and finally dissolved in the soul-searching affectations of Mannerism.

The Italian people had seen glorious days at the crossroads between East and West, and the growth of their city-states into great centers of vast wealth and sparkling culture. With strong spirit, they had survived the depredations of plague, war, and internal strife. But they had also seen the dream of communal republican governments evolve into dictatorships, whose jealousy and rivalry invited domination from the outside. At the end, the Italian Renaissance simply eroded, then faded away, leaving an artistic, political, and cultural afterimage that even today provides standards of excellence in the modern world.

Afterimage

The Renaissance in Italy was a time of great change. All aspects of life—social, religious, economic, cultural, and personal—underwent dramatic transformation. In many ways, historian Jacob Burckhardt is correct when he writes that the Renaissance was the birth of the modern world. As the people of the Italian Renaissance worked to solve the problems of daily life, they redefined the world in which they lived. Many of their solutions to the problems of their day have continued to be part of the twentieth century.

Products of the Renaissance

In today's commerce, numerous practices reflect the economic innovations of the Renaissance. Bankers still give loans and finance individual projects. Insurance companies, which during the Renaissance protected shipowners, have expanded their coverage to health, natural disasters, and accidents. Large companies still insure themselves against human-caused and natural events that would destroy their businesses. Today businesses and suppliers of goods and services offer credit to their customers as a commonplace. All of these practices had their start in the early Renaissance, when the needs of traders and merchants emerged as a defining element of society.

In politics, nearly every nation in the world has resident embassies that house diplomats and ambassadors. Rhetoric is still an important tool of politicians who run for office and seek to gain support for their policies and plans. Civic responsibility, even today, is lauded by idealists who believe that the duty of elected officials is to promote the welfare and stability of the populations they serve. These ideals, given voice by men like Petrarch and Boccaccio, have remained strong over the centuries.

Education, in both public and private schools, retains elements of the humanist program developed in the early Renaissance. Students study history, language, grammar, and, sometimes, rhetoric in schoolrooms throughout the world. Liberal arts study, though the content is slightly different than it was during the Renaissance, still forms the foundation of undergraduate programs in universities, and is part of the standard fare in elementary, middle, and high schools throughout the world. Students still read Aristotle, Plato, Cicero, and Livy as avidly as did men like Petrarch, Ficino, Mirandola, and Bruni.

One of the first lessons art students learn is the rules of perspective discovered by Brunelleschi and expanded by Leonardo da Vinci. In classrooms throughout the world, slides of the works of Masaccio, Donatello, Botticelli, Leonardo, Michelangelo, and Raphael are shown to students, and are held up as standards in representational art. Every year thousands of people travel to Florence and Rome to see these works, which have survived the ravages of time, the violence of war, and natural disasters. The art of the Renaissance is still some of the best loved in the Western world, not only because it is a source of pride and history, but because it still fills the viewer with awe.

Capital cities throughout the Western world boast domes that are direct descendants of Brunelleschi's architectural masterpiece. Today, just as in 1436, this architectural feature is a symbol of power, stability, and civic pride. Classical lines, balance, and proportion still provide the aesthetic ideals for many architects. Great columns and other functional and decorative elements, which had their beginnings in ancient times and were resurrected in the Renaissance, can today be seen on many buildings, public and private.

Men and women, young and old, have come to accept that the quest for human excellence is not at odds with the love of God. To choose work that is appropriate to one's abilities and preferences is the goal of many. To do one's work to the best of one's ability in the service of oneself, one's fellow humans, and one's God is now accepted as a matter of fact. This quest for excellence, taken for granted today, is a product of the civic humanism be-

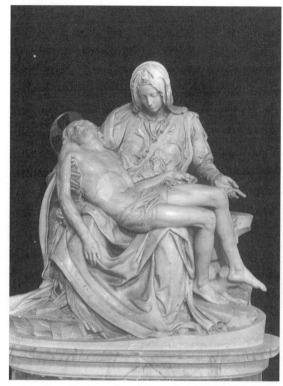

Today, people across the globe remain awed by the extraordinary products of the Renaissance, such as Michelangelo's emotionally compelling Pieta.

gun by Petrarch through his respect for ancient writers such as Cicero.

Though people in different times have modified the discoveries of the Renaissance to meet the evolving needs of a changing society, the glory of the past is still very much alive in the way we, in the twentieth century, view and build our world. Much of what we prize as the best in ourselves and our culture had its beginnings in a small country at the foot of Europe where human beings discovered the art and joy of being human.

Notes

Introduction: A Bridge in Time

1. Giovanni Pico della Mirandola, "Oration on the Dignity of Man," in Ernst Cassirer et al., eds., *The Renaissance Philosophy of Man*. Chicago: University of Chicago Press, 1948.

2. Quoted in James Bruce Ross and Mary Martin McLaughlin, eds., *The Portable Renaissance Reader*. Mary Martin McLaughlin, trans. New York: Viking, 1962.

Chapter 1: The Seeds of the Italian Renaissance

3. Quoted in James Bruce Ross and Mary Martin McLaughlin, eds., *The Portable Medieval Reader*. New York: Penguin, 1977.

4. De Lamar Jensen, *Renaissance Europe: Age of Discovery and Reconciliation*. 2nd ed. Lexington, MA: Heath, 1992.

5. Quoted in Anthony Bonner, ed. and trans., *Songs of the Troubadours*. New York: Schocken, 1972.

6. James A. Brundage, *The Crusades: A Documentary Survey*. Milwaukee: Marquette University Press, 1962.

7. John P. McKay, Bennett D. Hill, and John Buckler, *A History of Western Society*, vol. 1. Boston: Houghton Mifflin, 1987.

8. Quoted in Lauro Martines, *Power and Imagination: City-States in Renaissance Italy*. New York: Knopf, 1979.

9. Quoted in Frederic Austin Ogg, ed., *A Source Book of Medieval History: Documents Illustrative of European Life and Institutions from the German Invasions to the Renaissance*. New York: American Book, 1935.

10. Boccaccio, *Decameron*. John Payne, trans. Revised by Charles S. Singleton. Berkeley: University of California Press, 1982.

11. Donald Kagan et. al., *The Western Heritage*, vol. 1. New York: Macmillan, 1991.

Chapter 2: The Early Renaissance in Florence

12. James Cleugh, *The Medici: A Tale of Fifteen Generations*. New York: Doubleday, 1975.

13. Quoted in Cleugh, *The Medici*.

14. Luca Landucci, *A Florentine Diary: From 1450 to 1516*. Alice de Rosen Jervis, trans. London: J. M. Dent & Sons, 1927.

15. Cleugh, *The Medici*.

16. Quoted in J. R. Hale, *Florence and the Medici: The Pattern of Control*. Plymouth, Great Britain: Thames and Hudson, 1977.

17. Gene Brucker, *Renaissance Florence*. Berkeley: University of California Press, 1983.

18. Quoted in L. R. Lind, ed. and trans., *Lyric Poetry of the Italian Renaissance*. New Haven: Yale University Press, 1954.

Chapter 3: Humanism in the Early Renaissance

19. Marvin Perry et al., *Western Civilization: Ideas, Politics, and Society*, 4th ed., vol. 1. Boston: Houghton Mifflin, 1992.

20. Pico della Mirandola, "Oration on the Dignity of Man."

21. Quoted in Jensen, *Renaissance Europe*.

22. Frederick B. Artz, *From the Renaissance to Romanticism: Trends in Style in Art, Literature, and Music, 1300–1830*. Chicago: University of Chicago Press, 1975.

23. Cicero, "On the Republic: The Dream of Scipio," R. H. Rice, trans., in *The Norton Anthology of World Masterpieces*, 4th ed., vol 1. New York: Norton, 1979.

24. Jensen, *Renaissance Europe*.

25. Quoted in James Harvey Robinson, *An Introduction to the History of Western Europe*, revised by James T. Shotwell. Boston: Ginn, 1946.

26. Brucker, *Renaissance Florence*.

27. Francesco Guicciardini, *The History of Italy*. Sidney Alexander, trans. New York: Collier, 1969.

Chapter 4: Art and Architecture of the Early Renaissance

28. Quoted in Gene Brucker, ed., *The Society of Renaissance Florence*. New York: Harper, 1971.

29. Giorgio Vasari, *The Lives of the Artists: Biographies of the Most Eminent Architects, Painters, and Sculptors of Italy*. Julia Conaway Bondanella and Peter Bondanella, trans. Oxford: Oxford University Press, 1991.

30. William Fleming, *Arts and Ideas*, 8th ed. Fort Worth: Holt, 1991.

31. Vasari, *The Lives of the Artists*.

32. Helen Gardner, *Art Through the Ages*, 8th ed. San Diego: Harcourt, 1986.

33. Landucci, *A Florentine Diary*.

34. Gardner, *Art Through the Ages*.

Chapter 5: Rome and French Invasions of Italy

35. Quoted in Peter Partner, *Renaissance Rome 1500–1559: A Portrait of a Society*. Berkeley: University of California Press, 1976.

36. Quoted in E. R. Chamberlin, *The World of the Italian Renaissance*. London: Allen, 1982.

37. J. H. Plumb, *The Italian Renaissance: A Concise Survey of Its History and Culture*. New York: Harper, 1961.

38. Charles L. Stinger, *The Renaissance in Rome*. Bloomington: Indiana University Press, 1985.

39. Jensen, *Renaissance Europe*.

40. Quoted in Partner, *Renaissance Rome*.

41. Plumb, *The Italian Renaissance*.

42. Partner, *Renaissance Rome*.

43. Hale, *Florence and the Medici*.

44. Niccolo Machiavelli, *The Prince and other Works*. Allan H. Gilbert, trans. New York: Farrar, 1946.

Chapter 6: Three Great Artists of the High Renaissance

45. E. H. Gombrich, *The Story of Art*, 15th ed. Englewood Cliffs, NJ: Prentice, 1990.

46. Gombrich, *The Story of Art*.

47. Quoted in Gardner, *Art Through the Ages*.

48. Quoted in Elizabeth Gilmore Holt, ed., *A Documentary History of Art*, vol 1. Garden City, NY: Doubleday, 1957.

49. Gardner, *Art Through the Ages*.

50. Robert N. Linscott, ed., *The Complete Poems and Selected Letters of Michelangelo*. Creighton Gilbert, trans. Princeton, NJ: Princeton University Press, 1963.

51. Quoted in Vasari, *The Lives of the Artists*.

52. Vasari, *The Lives of the Artists*.

53. Quoted in Michael de Luca and William Giuliano, eds., *Selections from Italian Poetry*. Irvington-on-Hudson, NY: Harvey House, 1966.

Chapter 7: The Late Renaissance

54. Kagan, *The Western Heritage*.

55. Quoted in Kagan, *The Western Heritage*.

56. Quoted in Vincent Cronin, *The Flowering of the Renaissance*. New York: Dutton, 1969.

57. Leonardo da Vinci, *Note-Books*. Edward McCurdy, trans. New York: Empire State, 1923.

For Further Reading

Jose Fernandez Arenas, *The Key to Renaissance Art.* The Key to Art series. Minneapolis, MN: Lerner Publications, 1990. Though this lovely book does include art from both Spain and northern Europe, it focuses primarily on the Italian Renaissance. Includes a large number of color reproductions of the works. Easy to read.

E. R. Chamberlin, *Everyday Life in Renaissance Times.* Drawings by Helen Nixon Fairfield. New York: Putnam and Sons, 1967. An easy-to-read description of the daily life of both the rich and the poor in Renaissance Europe. Includes chapters on such diverse topics as science, witchcraft, and the plague.

Alison Cole, *Perspective: A Visual Guide to the Theory and Techniques—from the Renaissance to Pop Art.* Eyewitness Art series. New York: Dorling Kindersley, 1992. Published in association with the National Gallery, London. An exceptional, easy-to-read exploration of perspective. Lavishly illustrated, this book also includes reproductions and photographs of works by Masaccio, Leonardo da Vinci, Brunelleschi, and other Renaissance artists.

Michael de Luca and William Giuliano, eds. *Selections from Italian Poetry.* Irvington-on-Hudson, NY: Harvey House, 1966. Though selections extend beyond the bounds of the Renaissance, this book offers several bonuses to the reader. It is bilingual and includes a key to Italian pronunciation. The English translations are easier to read than most.

Henry S. Gillette, *Raphael: Painter of the Renaissance.* New York: Franklin Watts, 1961. An easy-to-read biography of the painter Raphael Santi. Includes black-and-white reproductions of many of his works.

Luca Landucci, *A Florentine Diary: From 1450 to 1516.* Alice de Rosen Jervis, trans. London: J. M. Dent & Sons, 1927. For the advanced reader, this is a wonderful primary source detailing the daily life of a Renaissance shopkeeper, who describes events both large and small from his own, very human, point of view.

Francesca Remei, *Leonardo da Vinci: Artist, Inventor, and Scientist of the Renaissance.* Ruth Nason, ed. Simon Knight, trans. Illustrated by Sergio and Andrea Ricciardi. New York: Peter Bedrick Books, 1994. Easy to read and liberally illustrated, this colorful and informative book explores Leonardo's personal life as well as his art, science, and inventions.

Marianne Sachs, *Leonardo and His World.* Morristown, NJ: Silver Burdett, 1980. This easy-to-read book places Leonardo and his works within the context of his world. A time line includes major events in Leonardo's life, which are given alongside other cultural and political events.

Irwin Shapiro, *The Golden Book of the Renaissance*. New York: Golden Press, 1962. A look at the art, people, and places of the Renaissance. Rich in detail and examples. Includes many illustrations and both black-and-white and color reproductions of artwork. Easy to read.

Author's Note: I also recommend the following films for their compelling depictions of events and individual accomplishments in the Renaissance. They are available on video.

The Agony and the Ecstasy (1965), directed by Carol Reed. Based on a novel by Irving Stone, starring Charlton Heston as Michelangelo and Rex Harrison as Pope Julius II. Not extremely accurate, but presents a very compelling story of the painting of the Sistine Chapel ceiling. Most importantly, it gives the viewer an accurate idea of the scope of Michelangelo's project.

Brother Sun, Sister Moon (1973), directed by Franco Zeffirelli, cowritten with Lina Wertmuller. Graham Faulkner as Francesco (Saint Francis) and Judi Bowker as Clare. A sensitive, beautifully filmed story based on the early life of Saint Francis of Assisi. Though slightly pre-Renaissance, this film gives the viewer an excellent feel for Italy, its merchants, its nobles, its poor, and its clergy. Strongly recommended.

Works Consulted

Oscar G. Brockett, *History of the Theatre.* 3rd ed. Boston: Allyn, 1977.

Howard M. Brown, *Music in the Renaissance.* History of Music Series. Englewood Cliffs, NJ: Prentice-Hall, 1976.

Jacob Burckhardt, *The Civilization of the Renaissance in Italy.* Introduction by Hajo Bolborn. S. G. C. Middlemore, trans. New York: Random House, 1954.

Peter Burke, *Culture and Society in Renaissance Italy.* London: Batsford, 1972.

John Calvin, *Tracts and Treatises in Defense of the Reformed Faith.* Vol. 3. Henry Beveridge, trans. Grand Rapids, MI: Wm. B. Eerdman's, 1958.

Ernst Cassirer et al., *The Renaissance Philosophy of Man.* Chicago: University of Chicago Press, 1948.

Richard of Devizes, Geoffrey de Vinsauf, and Lord John de Joinville, *Chronicles of the Crusades.* Henry G. Bohn, ed. London: Cox, 1848.

Charles Diehl, *Byzantium: Greatness and Decline.* Naomi Walford, trans. New Brunswick, NJ: Rutgers University Press, 1957.

Marsilio Ficino, *The Book of Life.* Charles Boer, trans. Dallas: Spring Publications, 1988.

Jefferson Butler Fletcher, *Literature of the Italian Renaissance.* Port Washington, NY: Kennikat Press, 1934.

Deno John Geanakoplos, *Interaction of the "Sibling" Byzantine and Western Cultures in the Middle Ages and Italian Renaissance (330–1600).* New Haven: Yale University Press, 1976.

Robert Goldwater and Marco Treves, eds., *Artists on Art: From the XIV to the XX Century.* New York: Pantheon, 1945.

Donald Jay Grout and Claude V. Palisca, *A History of Western Music.* 4th ed. New York: Norton, 1988.

Francesco Guicciardini, *The History of Italy and The History of Florence.* Cecil Grayson, trans. John R. Hale, ed. New York: Twayne, 1964.

George Holmes, *The Florentine Enlightenment.* New York: Oxford University Press, 1992.

Judith Hook, *Lorenzo de' Medici: An Historical Biography.* London: Hamish Hamilton, 1984.

Julian Klaczko, *Rome and the Renaissance: The Pontificate of Julius II.* John Dennie, trans. New York: Putnam, 1926.

John Larner, *Culture and Society in Italy 1290–1420.* New York: Scribner's, 1971.

Archibald R. Lewis, *Naval Power and Trade in the Mediterranean A.D. 500–1100.*

Princeton: Princeton University Press, 1951.

Michael Mallett, *Mercenaries and Their Masters: Warfare in Renaissance Italy*. London: The Bodley Head, 1974.

Lauro Martines, *The Social World of the Florentine Humanists 1390–1460*. Princeton: Princeton University Press, 1963.

Erskine Muir, *Machiavelli and His Times*. London: William Heinemann, 1936.

Brian Pullan, *A History of Early Renaissance Italy: From the Mid-Thirteenth to the Mid-Fifteenth Century*. London: Allen Lane, 1973.

Karl F. Thompson, ed., *Classics of Western Thought: Middle Ages, Renaissance, and Reformation*. 3rd ed. Vol 2. New York: Harcourt Brace Jovanovich, 1980.

Pasquale Villari, *Life and Times of Girolamo Savonarola*. Linda Villari, trans. London: T. Fisher Unwin, 1896.

Works Cited

Leon Battista Alberti, *On Painting.* John R. Spencer, trans. New Haven: Yale University Press, 1956. A Renaissance work considered to be the first modern treatise on painting theory. Difficult reading.

Frederick B. Artz, *From the Renaissance to Romanticism: Trends in Style in Art, Literature, and Music, 1300–1830.* Chicago: University of Chicago Press, 1975. Explores impulses in art, literature, and music from 1300 to 1830. Difficult reading.

Boccaccio, *Decameron.* John Payne, trans. Revised by Charles S. Singleton. Berkeley: University of California Press, 1982. A literary classic in which a group of young people tell one another stories to lessen the tediousness of confinement during the 1348 plague. Difficult reading.

Anthony Bonner, ed. and trans., *Songs of the Troubadours.* New York: Schocken, 1972. A scholarly study of the troubadours and the context in which they created their works. Difficult reading.

Gene Brucker, *Renaissance Florence.* Berkeley: University of California Press, 1983. A scholarly assessment of economic, social, and artistic trends in Florence during the early Renaissance. Difficult reading.

Gene Brucker, ed., *The Society of Renaissance Florence.* New York: Harper, 1971. A collection of primary source material, including letters, diary excerpts, and institutional proceedings of the early Renaissance in Florence. Difficult reading.

————, *Two Memoirs of Renaissance Florence: The Diaries of Buonaccorso Pitti and Gregorio Dati.* Julia Martines, trans. New York: Harper, 1967. Primary source accounts of the early Renaissance, written by two businessmen of the time. Vibrant and exciting for the advanced reader.

James A. Brundage, *The Crusades: A Documentary Survey.* Milwaukee: Marquette University Press, 1962. A collection of primary source material with commentary by Brundage. Advanced to difficult reading.

Baldassare Castiglione, *The Book of the Courtier.* L. E. Opdycke, trans. New York: Scribners, 1903. Renaissance author offers advice on how to become the ideal gentleman. Advanced reading.

E. R. Chamberlin, *The World of the Italian Renaissance.* London: Allen, 1982. A scholarly look at the evolution of the Renaissance and the components of its primary characteristics. Special emphasis on Florence, Rome, and Venice. Advanced reading.

James Cleugh, *The Medici: A Tale of Fifteen Generations.* New York: Doubleday, 1975. Follows the fortunes of Italy's most famous banking family from the late thirteenth century to the early eighteenth century. Difficult reading.

Vincent Cronin, *The Flowering of the Renaissance.* New York: Dutton, 1969.

Explores the politics and culture of the Renaissance from its height to its demise. Focuses strongly on Florence, Venice, Rome, and the evolution of Christian humanism. Difficult reading.

Leonardo da Vinci, *Note-Books*. Edward McCurdy, trans. New York: Empire State, 1923. A selection of writings from the personal notebooks of the famous painter. Focuses primarily on philosophical, artistic, and literary entries. Minimal number of sketches. Fascinating advanced to difficult reading.

Will Durant, *The Reformation: A History of European Civilization from Wyclif to Calvin: 1300–1564*. Part VI of *The Story of Civilization*. New York: Simon and Schuster, 1957. An in-depth study of the people and events of the Reformation. Includes many primary source references. Difficult reading.

————, *The Renaissance: A History of Civilization in Italy from 1304–1576 A.D.* Part V of *The Story of Civilization*. New York: Simon and Schuster, 1953. An encompassing look at Renaissance people, politics, culture, art, and economics. Primary source material included. Difficult reading.

Marsilio Ficino, *The Letters of Marsilio Ficino*. Vol. 2. Translated by the Language Department of the School of Economic Science, London. London: Shepheard-Walwyn, 1978. A collection of letters written by one of the most important humanists of the Renaissance. Rich in content and style. Difficult reading.

William Fleming, *Arts and Ideas*. 8th ed. Fort Worth: Holt, 1991. A humanities survey that explores the arts of the West and their contexts from ancient times to the late twentieth century. Highly illustrated. Difficult reading.

Frank Roy Fraprie, *The Raphael Book*. Boston: L. C. Page, 1912. An interesting account of Raphael's life, times, and paintings. Includes reproductions of the artist's work. Advanced reading.

James Anthony Froude, *The Life and Letters of Erasmus: Lectures Delivered at Oxford 1893–4*. London: Longman's Green, 1899. A collection of Erasmus's writings with commentary and some abridgment by Froude. Offers insight into the life of one of the most lively critics of the Renaissance church. Difficult reading.

Helen Gardner, *Art Through the Ages*. 8th ed. San Diego: Harcourt, 1986. A highly respected historical survey of art from its beginnings to the twentieth century. Difficult reading.

E. H. Gombrich, *The Story of Art*. 15th ed. Englewood Cliffs, NJ: Prentice, 1990. An historical survey of art from its beginnings to the first half of the twentieth century. Advanced reading.

Florence Alden Gragg, trans., and Leona C. Gabel, ed., *The Commentaries of Pius II*. Book III of Smith College Studies in History. Vol XXV. 1–4. Northampton, MA: Department of History of Smith College, 1939–40. Primary source commentaries on events of the Renaissance as experienced by one in power. Difficult reading.

Francesco Guicciardini, *The History of Italy*. Sidney Alexander, trans. New York:

Collier, 1969. Covers the history of Italy from 1492 to 1534, dates which fall within the author's life span. Difficult reading.

———, *The History of Italy and The History of Florence.* Cecil Grayson, trans. John R. Hale, ed. New York: Twayne, 1964. Includes Florentine history from 1378 to 1509. Difficult reading.

J. R. Hale, *Florence and the Medici: The Pattern of Control.* Plymouth, Great Britain: Thames and Hudson, 1977. This scholarly work explores the relationship between the Medici and the city they came to control. Difficult reading.

Henry Hart, *Marco Polo: Venetian Adventurer.* Norman: University of Oklahoma Press, 1967. A scholarly work describing the life of the famous thirteenth-century traveler. Rich in detail. Includes primary source references. Advanced reading.

Elizabeth Gilmore Holt, ed., *A Documentary History of Art.* Vol. 1. Garden City, NY: Doubleday, 1957. A collection of primary source material relating to the visual arts of the Middle Ages and the Renaissance. Some commentary. Advanced to difficult reading.

De Lamar Jensen, *Renaissance Europe: Age of Discovery and Reconciliation.* 2nd ed. Lexington, MA: Heath, 1992. A solid history of the Renaissance and its manifestations in both Italy and northern Europe. Advanced reading.

Donald Kagan et al., *The Western Heritage.* Vol 1. New York: Macmillan, 1991. A survey of Western history from Pale-

olithic times to the early eighteenth century. Difficult reading.

L. R. Lind, ed. and trans., *Lyric Poetry of the Italian Renaissance.* New Haven: Yale University Press, 1954. A bilingual anthology of Italian poetry from the early thirteenth to the late sixteenth century. Includes short biographies of poets. Advanced reading.

Robert N. Linscott, ed., *The Complete Poems and Selected Letters of Michelangelo.* Creighton Gilbert, trans. Princeton: Princeton University Press, 1963. Collected documents written by one of the most famous artists in history. Difficult reading.

Niccolo Machiavelli, *History of Florence: From the Earliest Times to the Death of Lorenzo the Magnificent.* New York: Colonial Press, 1901. The history of Italy and Florence from 379 to 1492 as interpreted by the most famous political theorist of the Renaissance. Difficult reading.

———, *The Prince and Other Works.* Allan H. Gilbert, trans. New York: Farrar, 1946. A Western classic of political theory written in 1513. Difficult reading.

Antonio di Tuccio Manetti, *The Life of Brunelleschi.* Catherine Enggass, trans. University Park: Pennsylvania State University Press, 1970. A fifteenth-century biography of the greatest architect of the Renaissance. Not always accurate. Difficult reading.

Lauro Martines, *Power and Imagination: City–States in Renaissance Italy.* New York: Knopf, 1979. A scholarly account of the people, politics, culture, and economics of Italy during the Renaissance. Difficult reading.

John P. McKay, Bennett D. Hill, and John Buckler, *A History of Western Society*. Vol. 1. Boston: Houghton Mifflin, 1987. An in-depth history of Western society from antiquity to the Enlightenment. Advanced reading.

Frederic Austin Ogg, ed., *A Source Book of Medieval History: Documents Illustrative of European Life and Institutions from the German Invasions to the Renaissance*. New York: American Book, 1935. Primary source material from the Middle Ages and early Renaissance. Includes commentary and explanation. Advanced to difficult reading.

Peter Partner, *Renaissance Rome 1500–1559: A Portrait of a Society*. Berkeley: University of California Press, 1976. An in-depth look at the history, economics, culture, and people of Renaissance Rome. Difficult reading.

Marvin Perry et al., *Western Civilization: Ideas, Politics, and Society*. 4th ed. Vol. 1. Boston: Houghton Mifflin, 1992. A historical survey of Western culture and history from ancient times to the Age of Enlightenment. Difficult reading.

Edward Peters, ed., *The First Crusade: The Chronicle of Fulcher of Chartres and other Source Material*. Philadelphia: University of Pennsylvania Press, 1971. A fascinating collection of primary source material covering Europe's First Crusade to the East. Advanced to difficult reading.

Giovanni Pico della Mirandola, "Oration on the Dignity of Man," in Ernst Cassirer et al., eds., *The Renaissance Philosophy of Man*. Chicago: University of Chicago Press, 1948. A classic essay on human nature written by one of the most prominent humanists of the Renaissance. Advanced reading.

J. H. Plumb, *The Italian Renaissance: A Concise Survey of Its History and Culture*. New York: Harper, 1961. The author's richly descriptive style separates this work from most other histories of the Renaissance. Advanced reading.

Gertrude Randolph Bramlette Richards, ed., *Florentine Merchants in the Age of the Medici: Letters and Documents from the Selfridge Collection of Medici Manuscripts*. Cambridge, MA: Harvard University Press, 1932. Selected translations of letters and documents relating to business as it was conducted by the Medici, their peers, and their representatives in the sixteenth and seventeenth centuries. Detailed primary source material for the advanced reader.

James Harvey Robinson, *An Introduction to the History of Western Europe*. Revised by James T. Shotwell. Boston: Ginn, 1946. A history of Europe from its beginnings in the Roman Empire to the eighteenth century. Includes primary source quotes. Advanced reading.

James Harvey Robinson, ed., *Readings in European History*. Vol. 2. Boston: Ginn, 1906. A collection of primary source material from Charles VIII's entry into Italy to the end of the nineteenth century, with commentary and explication by the editor. Difficult reading.

James Harvey Robinson and H. W. Rolfe, trans. *Petrarch, the First Modern Scholar and Man of Letters.* New York: Putnam, 1898. Selected writings of Petrarch. Includes commentary. Advanced to difficult reading.

James Bruce Ross and Mary Martin McLaughlin, eds., *The Portable Medieval Reader.* New York: Penguin, 1977. A collection of primary source material from the Middle Ages. Selections range from advanced to difficult reading.

———, *The Portable Renaissance Reader.* Mary Martin McLaughlin, trans. New York: Viking, 1962. A collection of primary source material from the European Renaissance. Selections range from advanced to difficult reading.

Charles L. Stinger, *The Renaissance in Rome.* Bloomington: Indiana University Press, 1985. A scholarly work focusing on the distinctive development of the Roman Renaissance. Takes into account political, social, economic, intellectual, and artistic factors. Difficult reading.

William Thomas, *The History of Italy.* George B. Parks, ed. Ithaca: Cornell University Press, 1963. Written by a Welshman who lived from 1507 to 1554 and traveled to Italy, this is regarded as the first book written about Italy in English. Difficult reading.

Giorgio Vasari, *The Lives of the Artists: Biographies of the Most Eminent Architects, Painters, and Sculptors of Italy.* Julia Conaway Bondanella and Peter Bondanella, trans. New York: Oxford University Press, 1991. A collection of Renaissance artists' biographies. Not always accurate, but written with charm and authority by one who lived during the Renaissance. Advanced reading.

Index

Achilles (Laschi), 53
aerial perspective, 49
Agricola, Alexander, 54
Alberti, Leon Battista, 25, 44
Albizzi, Luca degli, 32
Albizzi, Piero degli, 32
Albizzi family, 28, 30
Albrecht (German
    archbishop), 83-84
Aldine Press, 40-41
Alexander VI (pope), 60, 62
Alfonso (king of Naples), 43
Alfonso II (king of Naples),
    64
Allesandri family, 41
Angiolieri, Cecco, 19
Ariosto, Lodovico, 54
Aristotle, 41, 92
art and architecture
    dome of Santa Maria del
        Fiore, 45-47
    early Renaissance, 44-55
    humanism and, 45-46
    music, 54-55
    patronage of, 44-45, 50-51,
        69-70
        by Medicis, 30-31
        trade guilds and, 44-45,
            53
    perspective
        aerial, 49
        linear, 47-49
    sculpture
        of early Renaissance,
            49-50
        of Michelangelo, 73-75
    theater, 52-54
Avignon Papacy, 21-22, 57, 83

banking, development of,
    17-19
Barbo, Pietro, 62

Benedict XI (pope), 21
Birth of Venus (Botticelli), 52
Black Death (bubonic
    plague), 23-24
Boccaccio, Giovanni, 23-25,
    35-36, 92
Boniface VIII (pope), 21
Boniface IX (pope), 57
Book of the Courtier, The,
    (Castiglione), 91
Borgia, Cesare, 60, 73
Borgia, Lucrezia, 60
Borgia, Rodrigo, 62
Botticelli, Sandro, 12, 32, 44,
    51-52, 93
Bound Slave (Michelangelo),
    73
Bracciolini, Poggio, 43, 56-57
Brunelleschi, Filippo, 25, 30,
    69
    dome of Santa Maria del
        Fiore, 45-47, 54
    linear perspective and,
        47-49, 93
Bruni, Leonardo, 25, 36-37,
    43, 92
bubonic plague (Black
    Death), 23-24
Burckhardt, Jacob, 12, 92

Caetani family, 57
Calvin, John, 90
Canale, Martinoda, 18
Casket, The (Ariosto), 54
Cassirer, Ernst, 37
Castiglione, Baldassare, 91
Catholic Church. *See* Roman
    Catholic Church
Charles I (king of Spain)
    becomes Holy Roman
        Emperor Charles V,
        85-87

Charles V (king of France),
    22
Charles VIII (king of
    France), 64-65
Chrysoloras, Manuel, 36
Cicero (ancient Roman
    orator), 35-36, 92-93
city-states, development of,
    13-14
classics (Greek/Roman)
    humanism and, 34-36
Clement V (pope), 21
Clement VII (pope), 22,
    86-87
Colonna family, 57
Columbus, Christopher, 81
Commentaries (Pius II), 63
Compere, Loyset, 54
Contessa, Bartolo della, 32
Copernicus, Nicolaus, 40
Corbinelli family, 41
Corbizi family, 32
Council of Trent, 87-88
courtly love, 15-16
Creation of Adam, The
    (Michelangelo), 77
Crusades, 16-17

Dante Alighieri, 16
Davanzati family, 41
David (Donatello), 50
David (Michelangelo), 73, 75
da Vinci, Leonardo. *See*
    Leonardo da Vinci
Decameron, The (Boccaccio),
    35
Dei, Benedetto, 26
Dias, Bartholomew, 82
dome of Santa Maria del
    Fiore, 45-47, 54
Donatello (sculptor), 25, 44,
    49-50, 93

Dufay, Guillaume, 25, 54
Dying Slave (Michelangelo), 73, 75

Eccerinus (Mussato), 53
education, changes in, 19-20
Embryo in the Womb (da Vinci), 71
Erasmus, Desiderius, 82, 90
Eugenius IV (pope), 47, 58

Ferantino (prince of Naples), 64
Ficino, Marsilio, 3, 12, 42, 92
Filocopo (Boccaccio), 35
Florence, Italy, in early Renaissance, 25-33
  location, importance of, 27
  Medici family's control of, 28-33, 64, 66-68
  merchants and bankers in, 27-28
Florentine Platonic Academy, 36-38, 51
Francis I (king of France), 66, 73, 85
Francis of Assisi, Saint, 20-21
Franco, Matteo, 33
Frederick III (emperor of Germany), 30
French invasions of Italy, 64-66

Gama, Vasco da, 82
Genevan Academy, 90-91
Ghiberti (sculptor), 30
Ghirlandaio, Domenico, 32, 69
Ghiselin, Johannes, 54
Giotto di Bondone, 23, 44, 47, 49, 69
Gozzoli, Benozzo, 30
Great Schism, 22, 57, 83
Gregory XI (pope), 21
Guicciardini, Francesco, 43
Gutenberg, Johannes, 40
High Renaissance, 68

fate of humanism, 90-91
great artists of, 69-80
Mannerism style, 89-90
papacy in trouble, 83-84
History of Florence (Machiavelli), 29
History of Italy, The (Guicciardini), 43
"holy wars" (the Crusades), 16-17
Horace (ancient Roman poet), 35
humanism, 11-12
  art and, 45-46
  classical study and, 34-36
  fate of, 90-91
  Florentine Platonic Academy and, 36-38, 51
  humanism elite, 41-43
  in the early Renaissance, 34-43
  medical study and, 38, 40
  Roman, 60-62

Inconstancy of Fortune, The (Bracciolini), 57
indulgences, 83-84, 88
Innocent III (pope), 20
Innocent VII (pope), 58, 60
Italian Renaissance
  faded away, 91
  important dates in, 8-9
  see also art and architecture;
    Florence, in early Renaissance;
    High Renaissance;
    humanism; Roman Catholic Church; Rome
Italy
  French invasions of, 64-66
  map of, during Renaissance, 13
  Turkish threat to, 62-64
  see also Italian Renaissance;
    Rome

John Paleologue (emperor of Byzantium), 30
Journey of the Magi (Gozzoli), 30
Julius II (pope), 59, 75-79

Lana guild, 45, 53
Landucci, Luca, 30, 50-51
Lapi family, 41, 50
Laschi, Antonio, 53
Last Supper, The (da Vinci), 71-72
late Renaissance, 81-91
Leonardo da Vinci, 10, 49, 79, 89, 93
  military engineering and, 72-73, 76
  paintings and notebooks of, 69-72
Leo X (pope), 60-61, 66, 79, 83, 85-86
  see also Medici, Giovanni de'
linear perspective, 47-49
Linscott, Robert N., 76
Livy (ancient Roman historian), 92
Louis XII (king of France), 64-66
Luther, Martin, 84-86, 90

Machiavelli, Niccolo, 29, 67-68
Madonna Goldfinch (Raphael), 78
Madonna of Cloth (Raphael), 78
Madonna with the Long Neck (Parmigianino), 89-90
madrigal(s), 54-55
Malatesta family, 54
Manetti, Antonio di Tucci, 48
Mannerism style, 89-90
Mannucci, Aldo, 40-41
map of Renaissance Italy, 13
marriages, arranged,

importance of, 18-19, 32
Marsuppini, Carlo, 43
Martin V (pope), 57-58
Martini, Johannes, 54
Masaccio (painter), 25, 44, 48-49, 69, 93
Maxmillian I (Holy Roman emperor), 85
medical study, and humanism, 38, 40
Medici, Cosimo de', 28-31, 37, 44
Medici, Giovanni de', 29, 60-61
    see also Leo X (pope)
Medici, Lorenzo de' (the Magnificent), 61
    art patronage by, 44, 51, 54, 70
    as poet, 33
    Florence under, 30-33
Medici, Lorenzo de' (Lorenzo the Magnificent's grandson), 66-68
Medici, Piero de' (Lorenzo the Magnificent's father), 31
Medici, Piero de' (Lorenzo the Magnificent's son), 66
Medici family, 50
    control of Florence, 28-33
        deposed by Charles VIII, 64
        return to control, 66-68
    patronage of arts and scholarship, 30-31
Melanchthon, Philip, 90
Memoirs (Philip of Commines), 65
Michelangelo Buonarroti, 69, 89, 93
    ceiling of Sistine Chapel, 10, 62, 76-77
    sculptures, 50, 73-75
    survived the High Renaissance, 79-80

Michelozzo (architect), 30
Middle Ages, 12
    the Church in, 19
middle class, rise of, 23-24
Mirandola. See Pico della Mirandola, Giovanni
Mona Lisa (da Vinci), 10, 72-73
Montefeltro family, 59
Moses (Michelangelo), 73
music, of early Renaissance, 54-55
Mussato, Albertino, 53

nepotism, 59-60
Nicholas V (pope), 60-61, 63
Ninety-five Theses (Luther), 84-85

On Painting (Alberti), 45
"Oration on the Dignity of God" (Pico della Mirandola), 11-12, 37
Oratory of Divine Love, 85
Otto of Freising, 13-14
Ovid (ancient Roman poet), 35

Pallas and the Centaur (Botticelli), 12
Papal States, 58-59
Parmigianino (painter), 89-90
patrons of art, 50-51, 69-70
    Medici family as, 30-31
    trade guilds and, 44-45, 53
Paul, Saint, 82
Paul II (pope), 62
Paul III (pope), 87-88
Paulus (Vergio), 53
Pazzi family, 30
Peace of Lodi, 63
perspective
    aerial, 49
    linear, 47-49
Perugino, Pietro, 32, 69

Peter, Saint, 59
Petrarch, Francesco, 16, 35-36, 39, 55, 92-93
Petrucci, Ottaviano de', 55
Philip IV (king of France), 21
Philip of Commines, 65
Pico della Mirandola, Giovanni, 11-12, 33-34, 37, 92
Pitti, Buonaccorso, 32
Pitti family, 50
Pius II (pope), 30, 61-63
Pius III (pope), 75
Plato, 37-38, 51, 92
Platonic Academy, Florentine, 36-38, 51
Prez, Josquin des, 54
Prince, The (Machiavelli), 67-68
printing press, impact of, 40-41

Quarguagli, Cerubino, 42

Rairio, Girolamo, 60
Rairio, Piero, 60
Raphael Santi, 49, 69, 74, 89, 93
    his temperament and works, 78-80
Reformation, Protestant, 84-86
Renaissance
    defined and described, 10-12
    late, 81-91
    products of, 92-93
    see also art and architecture; Florence, Italy, in early Renaissance; High Renaissance; humanism; Italian Renaissance; Roman Catholic Church; Rome
Robert the Monk, 21

Roman Academy, 53
Roman Catholic Church
    Avignon papacy and Great
        Schism and, 21-23, 57, 83
    Council of Trent, 87-88
    indulgences and, 83-84, 88
    Luther and the
        Reformation, 84-86
    nepotism in, 59-60, 83-84
    papacy, in trouble, 83-84
    reform movements in,
        20-21
    simony in, 83, 87
    status in Middle Ages, 19
Rome, 56-64
    as city in trouble, 56-58
    humanism in, 60-62
    Papal States and, 58-59
    pomp of, 88
    sack of, 85-87
    Turkish threat to, 62-64
    see also Roman Catholic
        Church
Rossi family, 41
Rovere, Giovanni della, 60

Rovere, Giuliano della, 59
    see also Julius II (pope)

sack of Rome, 85-87
Salutati, Colluccio, 43
Santa Maria del Fiore, dome
    of, 45-47, 54
Savelli family, 57
Savonarola, Girolamo, 64,
    66-67
School of Athens (Raphael), 79
sculpture
    of early Renaissance, 49-50
    of Michelangelo, 73-75
Sforza, Ludovico, 64-66
Sforza family, 54-59
simony, 83-84, 87
Sistine Chapel, ceiling of,
    10, 62, 76-77
Sixtus IV (pope), 59, 62
Sophocles (ancient Greek
    playwright), 41
Spinelli family, 41, 50
St. Mark (Donatello), 49
Strozzi family, 41, 50

Teseide (Boccaccio), 35
theater, of early Renaissance,
    52-54
time line of Italian
    Renaissance, 8-9
trade guilds
    art patronage and, 44-45,
        53
Turks, as threat to Italy, 62-64

Urban II (pope), 21
Urban VI (pope), 21-22

Valla, Lorenzo, 43
Vasari, Giorgio, 23, 45, 47, 78
Vergio, Pier Paolo, 53
Verrocchio, Andrea del, 69
Vinci, Leonardo da. See
    Leonardo da Vinci
Virgil, 35

Weerbeke, Gaspar van, 54

Picture Credits

Cover photo by SCALA/Art Resource

Alinari/Art Resource, 30, 46 (top), 50, 58, 75 (both), 79 (top), 93

Archive Photos, 36, 39, 67, 71

The Bettmann Archive, 33, 35, 38, 60, 62, 65

Giraudon/Art Resource, 66

Library of Congress, 22, 40, 41, 68, 81, 84, 85 (both)

North Wind Picture Archives, 26, 31, 87

Planet Art, 10, 12, 51 (right), 52, 70 (both), 73, 77, 78 (both), 79 (bottom)

SCALA/Art Resource, 49, 90

About the Author

Karen Osman is currently working on a Ph.D. in fine arts, which includes study in theater, music, the visual arts, and philosophy. She has written *Gangs* for Lucent's Overview Series, as well as numerous plays, short stories, humor articles, and videos. Her academic credits include presentations to the American Society for Aesthetics and the Association for Theatre in Higher Education.